OECD Studies on Water

Fostering Water Resilience in Brazil

TURNING STRATEGY INTO ACTION

This document, as well as any data and map included herein, are without prejudice to the status of or sovereignty over any territory, to the delimitation of international frontiers and boundaries and to the name of any territory, city or area.

Please cite this publication as:
OECD (2022), *Fostering Water Resilience in Brazil: Turning Strategy into Action*, OECD Studies on Water, OECD Publishing, Paris, *https://doi.org/10.1787/85a99a7c-en*.

ISBN 978-92-64-54494-9 (print)
ISBN 978-92-64-54375-1 (pdf)

OECD Studies on Water
ISSN 2224-5073 (print)
ISSN 2224-5081 (online)

Photo credits: Cover © Getty/TacioPhilip

Corrigenda to publications may be found on line at: *www.oecd.org/about/publishing/corrigenda.htm*.
© OECD 2022

The use of this work, whether digital or print, is governed by the Terms and Conditions to be found at *http://www.oecd.org/termsandconditions*.

Preface

Enhancing water resilience is urgent in Brazil, where nearly 100 million people lack access to safe sanitation. In addition, over 200 million rely on hydropower for two-thirds of their electricity, further reinforcing the importance of resilience, especially given the increasing intensity and frequency of extreme water-related events such as floods and droughts.

This report builds on a decade of policy dialogues between the OECD and the National Water and Sanitation Agency (ANA) of Brazil, which delivered the studies *Water Resources Governance in Brazil* (2015) and *Water Charges in Brazil: the Ways Forward* (2017). It provides practical, action-oriented guidance to strengthen water resilience in light of two recent institutional and policy changes: first, the implementation of the 2019 National Water Security Plan containing strategic infrastructure requirements and an investment plan to 2035; and second, the Federal Sanitation Law 14.206/2020, which expanded ANA's portfolio beyond water resources management to include sanitation prerogatives.

Four workshops involving 200+ stakeholders over the period 2019-21 informed this report. The first addressed strategic issues on Upgrading, Governing and Financing Water Infrastructure (14-18 October 2019). The second looked at Regulating Water Management across Levels of Government (19-22 October 2020). The third (25-28 May 2021) and fourth workshops (21-24 September 2021) focused on the Piancó-Piranhas Açu River Basin to discuss respectively River Basin Governance, and Water Allocation Regimes and Economic Instruments. This report also benefitted from the experience of peer reviewers from Australia, the European Commission, France, Italy, Spain, the United Kingdom and the United States.

The report calls for a modern approach to water security, balancing supply and demand management, grey and green infrastructure, and risk management and resilience while embracing a holistic view that connects water to other strategic areas such as environment, land use and territorial development. The report further notes that the conservation of water ecosystems should be enhanced to guarantee water availability for all needs in the long term. Moreover, high urbanisation rates in Brazil highlight the need to better integrate territorial development and water resources management policies. Finally, land use directly affects the magnitude of extreme water-related events such as floods, especially for vulnerable people, calling for coordination across levels of government, conducive regulation and adequate economic instruments.

The OECD stands ready to continue supporting Brazil in advancing water policies for better lives.

Lamia Kamal-Chaoui
Director, Centre for Entrepreneurship,
SMEs, Regions and Cities, OECD

Christianne Dias Ferreira
Director-President of the ANA

Foreword

Fostering Water Resilience in Brazil: Turning Strategy into Action builds on the policy recommendations set out in the OECD reports *Water Resources Governance in Brazil* (2015) and *Water Charges in Brazil* (2017), and four multi-stakeholder, capacity-building workshops carried out over the period 2019-21 to learn from the state-of-the-art and international best practices.

The report is the last of a series of OECD Studies on Water carried out in Latin American countries, such as in Mexico (2013), Argentina (2019) and Peru (2021). The report focuses on improving multi-level governance and financing to enhance water resilience in Brazil and cope with pressing and emerging environmental, economic and social challenges.

Previous OECD reports show that Brazil made significant progress in managing water resources since the adoption of the National Water Law in 1997 and the creation of the National Water and Sanitation Agency (ANA) in 2000. Nevertheless, water security challenges persist and will be aggravated by megatrends such as climate change, population growth, and urbanisation, and indeed potentially exacerbated by longer-term economic, social and environmental consequences of the COVID-19 pandemic, including constraints on public finances. In 2020, 1.1 million Brazilians were affected by floods and 15.8 million by droughts. Currently, 95.2 million people lack access to safe sanitation, and 2.3 million people use unsafe water sources for consumption and for personal and domestic hygiene.

In response to these challenges, Brazil has raised the profile of water security in its political agenda over the past decades, strengthening the link between water management and territorial development, and shaping an investment plan of BRL 27.6 billion to 2035. At the same time, the New Sanitation Law adopted in 2020 encourages transparency, allowing private investors to contribute to the goal of universal access to safe drinking water and sanitation. The action-oriented guidance provided in this report aims to support Brazil to: (1) move from a risk-based to a resilience approach that responds to megatrends such as climate change, demographic growth and urbanisation; (2) use economic instruments at basin level and strengthen multi-level governance; and (3) improve regulatory oversight and monitoring.

Acknowledgements

This report was prepared by the Centre for Entrepreneurship, SMEs, Regions and Cities (CFE), led by Lamia Kamal-Chaoui, in co-operation with the Environment Directorate (ENV), led by Rodolfo Lacy, and the Public Governance Directorate (GOV), led by Elsa Pilichowski. It summarises the findings of four capacity building workshops carried out by the OECD Secretariat in co-operation with the National Water and Sanitation Agency (ANA) of Brazil between 2019 and 2021 with 200+ stakeholders from the public, private and non-profit sectors to discuss the implementation of policy recommendations from previous OECD reports on water governance (2015) and financing (2017). The workshops' themes were: Upgrading, Governing and Financing Water Infrastructure (14-18 October 2019), Regulating Water Management Across Levels of Government (19-22 October 2020), Strengthening River Basin Governance in the Piancó-Piranhas Açu River Basin (25-28 May 2021) and Strengthening Water Allocation Regimes and Economic Instruments in the Piancó-Piranhas Açu River Basin (21-24 September 2021).

The OECD Secretariat thanks the following ANA team members for the excellent co-operation: Oscar Cordeiro Netto, Tauana Monteiro, Patrick Thomas, Alan Vaz, Humberto Gonçalves, Nazareno Araujo and Mariana Schneider; as well as ANA officials who participated in the workshops and contributed with their presentations and inputs, namely: Christianne Dias, Marcelo Cruz, Ricardo Andrade, Joaquim Gondim, Gisela Forattini, Flávia Barros, Tibério Pinheiro, Carlos Perdigão, Sérgio Ayrimoraes, Ana Fioreze, Carlos Motta, Cíntia Araújo, Flávia Carneiro, Bruna Craveiro, José Zoby, Elizabeth Juliatto, Carolina Arantes, Cristianny Teixeira, Marcelo Pires, Giordano Carvalho, Marcelo Mazzola as well as Flávio Tröger and André Pante. We also acknowledge the participation of Brazilian speakers and contributors to the Workshops, namely: Jerson Kelman, Martha Seillier, Manoel Renato, Sérgio Costa, Mariana Andrade, Rafael Teza, Cristiane Battiston, Fabiano Pompermayer, Alexandre Godeiro, Verônica Sánchez, Irani Braga, Ernani Miranda, Jorge Werneck, Gabriel Fiuza, Laura Bedeschi, Leticia Barbosa, Alceu Galvão, Percy Soares Neto, Wladimir Ribeiro, Paulo Varella, Procópio Lucena, Geny Formiga, Francisco Auricélio, Porfírio Loureiro, Bruno Rebouças, Marcilio Caetano, Stela Goldestein, Thadeu Abicalil, Gilberto Canali and Guilherme Marques.

The report and related workshops were coordinated by Oriana Romano, Head of the CFE Water Governance and Circular Economy Unit, under the supervision of Aziza Akhmouch, Head of the CFE Cities, Urban Policies and Sustainable Development Division, in co-operation with Anna Pietikainen, GOV Senior Policy Advisor, and Gerard Bonnis, ENV Senior Policy Analyst. The report was drafted by a team comprising: Ian Barker, founder and Managing Director of Water Policy International Ltd. (Chapter 1); Gerard Bonnis, Senior Policy Analyst, and Delia Sanchez Trancon, Junior Economist, both in ENV, and Maria Salvetti, Senior Economist in CFE (Chapter 2); and Anna Pietikainen, Senior Policy Advisor, Martha Baxter and Ana Simion, Policy Analysts in GOV (Chapter 3). Kathleen Dominique, Senior Policy Analyst (ENV) and Guillaume Gruère, Head of Unit, Climate change, Environment and Resources (Trade and Agriculture Directorate, TAD) provided inputs during Workshop 4. Ander Eizaguirre, Mélissa Kerim-Dikeni and Juliette Lassman, Junior Policy Analysts in CFE, provided inputs to Chapters 1 and 2, and contributed to the organisation of the online workshops.

The workshops benefitted from contributions by the following peer reviewers and experts who shared their country's experience with Brazilian stakeholders: Ian Barker, founder and Managing Director, Water Policy International Ltd., United Kingdom; Sanford Berg, Professor Emeritus of Economics, University of Florida, US; Sandrine Dupuis, Head of Water Charges at the Adour Garonne Water Agency, France; Peter Gammeltoft, former Head of Unit for Water at the Directorate General for the Environment, European Commission; Joseph Glauber, Senior Research Fellow at the International Food Policy Research Institute (IFPRI); Quentin Grafton, Professor of Economics and UNESCO Chair in Water Economics and Transboundary Water Governance at the Australian National University, Australia; Michael Hanemann, Professor of Economics at the W. P. Carey School of Business; Marit Hjort, Programme Analyst at the United Nations Development Programme; Patrick Laigneau, Senior Water Management Expert, France; Jay Lund, Professor of Civil and Environmental Engineering, US; Fernando Magdaleno Mas, Senior Coordinator, General Water Directorate, Ministry for Ecological Transition, Spain; Sharon Megdal, Director of the University of Arizona Water Resources Research Center, US; Christian Minelli, European and International External Relations, Regulatory Authority for Energy, Networks and Environment, Italy; David Satti, Assistant Director, Water Industry Commission for Scotland (WICS); Laura Tanco Ballesteros, Hydrological Planning Office of the Jucar Basin Organisation, Spain; and Adam Wilson, Chief Executive Officer, Essential Services Commission of South Australia, Australia.

The report was submitted for approval by written procedure to the Regional Development Policy Committee (RDPC) on 9 December 2021 under the cote CFE/RDPC/WGI(2021)4. It was also submitted to the delegates of the Network of Economic Regulators (NER) and the Working Party on Biodiversity, Water and Ecosystems (WPBWE) for comments. The final version was edited by Misha Pinkhasov and formatted by Eleonore Morena. François Iglesias and Pilar Philip prepared the manuscript for publication.

Table of contents

Preface	3
Foreword	4
Acknowledgements	5
Executive summary	11
1 Governing water infrastructure for greater resilience	**13**
Infrastructure for water security in Brazil	14
Getting the governance of water infrastructure right	17
Enhancing coordination across levels of government	17
Aiming for resilience	19
Ensuring policy coherence	20
Building capacities	21
Improving data collection and analysis	23
Funding the multi-purpose operation and maintenance of water infrastructure	24
Developing demand management	27
Engaging stakeholders	28
References	29
Annex 1.A. Action plan	31
Note	33
2 Strengthening multi-level governance and the use of economic instruments in the Piancó-Piranhas Açu River Basin	**35**
Hydrological features of the Piancó-Piranhas Açu basin	36
Increasing water security through the São Francisco Integration Project	38
Getting water governance right in the Piancó-Piranhas Açu River Basin	44
Adopting a governance arrangement that ensures water management at an appropriate scale and fosters coordination	44
Strengthening stakeholder engagement	47
Investing in monitoring and hydrology control	51
Improving water allocation mechanisms	52
Environmental Flows	55
Compensation mechanisms	56
Strengthening economic instruments in the Piancó-Piranhas Açu river basin	59
Pricing and financing of integrated water resources management in the PPA basin	59
Financing the operation and maintenance of water storage and transport infrastructure	60
Implementing the principle of water pays for water	63

Promoting efficient water use	69
Combining policy instruments	72
Abstraction charges and water markets	73
Abstraction charges and direct regulation	74
Water markets and direct regulation	75
References	76
Annex 2.A. Action plan	79
Notes	80

3 Making water and sanitation regulation in Brazil more effective 81

The 2020 sanitation law	82
Making the reform effective	84
Achieving role clarity	84
Coordinating effectively	88
Defining an adequate transition period and managing expectations of ANA	89
Building adequate human and technical capacities	90
Achieving effective oversight and enforcement	92
Ensuring effective stakeholder engagement	95
Decentralising to achieve better regulatory outcomes	97
Planning infrastructure and involving the private sector in WSS	99
Understanding finance providers' perspectives	102
References	103
Annex 3.A. Action plan	105
Notes	106

Annex A. List of stakeholders consulted during the workshops 107

Tables

Table 1.1. Green Infrastructure solutions for water resource management	18
Table 2.1. OECD principles of stakeholder engagement for inclusive water governance	48
Table 2.2. Brazil's water allocation regime	54
Table 2.3. Water abstraction rates in the Adour-Garonne basin	68
Table 2.4. Volume abstracted and charging of abstractions in the Adour-Garonne basin	68
Table 2.5. Pollution charge for domestic users in the Adour-Garonne River Basin, France	69
Table 2.6. Pollution charge for non-domestic users in the Adour-Garonne River Basin, France	69
Table 3.1. Main changes to ANA roles and responsibilities in the 2020 Sanitation Law	83
Table 3.2. WSS framework and actors involved	85
Table 3.3. Scope of action and independence of ARERA	86

Annex Table 1.A.1. Governing water infrastructure for greater resilience	31
Annex Table 2.A.1. Strengthening multi-level governance and the use of economic instruments in the Piancó-Piranhas Açu River Basin	79
Annex Table 3.A.1. Making water and sanitation regulation in Brazil more effective	105

Figures

Figure 1.1. OECD Principles on Water Governance	16
Figure 2.1. The Piancó-Piranhas Açu River Basin	36
Figure 2.2. Reservoir systems in the Piancó-Piranhas Açu River Basin	37
Figure 2.3. Water use in the Piancó-Piranhas Açu River Basin, per sector	38
Figure 2.4. Northern and eastern routes of the São Francisco water transfer project	39
Figure 2.5. Institutional mapping for water resources management in the Piancó-Piranhas Açu River Basin, Brazil	46

Figure 2.6. Conceptual framework for the pricing and financing of integrated water resources management in the PPA basin 60
Figure 2.7. Financing O&M of bulk water infrastructure in the PPA basin 62
Figure 2.8. Abstraction charges, water allocation and IWRM: a multifaceted interface 66
Figure 2.9. Combining an abstraction charge with a tradable permit system to address water scarcity hot spots 74
Figure 2.10. Cost-efficiency of a combination of abstraction charge and direct regulation 75
Figure 3.1. Evolution of the role of ANA 82
Figure 3.2. Water and Sanitation data – a snapshot for Brazil (2018) 84
Figure 3.3. Scope of regulatory action in WAREG 87
Figure 3.4. Job families in water regulatory agencies 91
Figure 3.5. ESCOSA business model 94
Figure 3.6. Stakeholder process triangle 96
Figure 3.7. Multi-level water governance in Italy 98
Figure 3.8. Core regulatory functions carried out by water regulators 99
Figure 3.9. OECD Recommendation on the Governance of Infrastructure 100

Boxes

Box 1.1. The OECD Principles on Water Governance 15
Box 1.2. Reaping the benefits of green infrastructure in the water sector 18
Box 1.3. Enhancing capacity at a sub-national level in the EU 22
Box 1.4. Financial support for water infrastructure in the EU 26
Box 1.5. International experience in moving from supply to demand management 27
Box 2.1. International experience of large water transfer schemes 42
Box 2.2. OECD principles of stakeholder engagement for inclusive water governance 47
Box 2.3. Cape Town's strategy for building resilience through partnership and collaboration 48
Box 2.4. The Fitzroy River Declaration for greater stakeholder engagement 49
Box 2.5. Monitoring and hydrological control in Spain, France and California, US 51
Box 2.6. 2015 OECD assessment and recommendations for water allocation in Brazil 52
Box 2.7. Options for treatment of in-stream flows within a water allocation regime 55
Box 2.8. Impacts of failing to consider environmental flows 56
Box 2.9. Agricultural risk management instruments 57
Box 2.10. Irrigators' tribunals on the Spanish Mediterranean coast 58
Box 2.11. 2017 OECD assessment and recommendations on water abstraction charges in Brazil 63
Box 2.12. Charging for water abstraction and discharges: A checklist 64
Box 2.13. Water abstraction charges in France 67
Box 2.14. Water markets in the western United States 71
Box 2.15. Water markets in the Murray–Darling Basin, Australia 72
Box 3.1. Independent regulation in Italy 86
Box 3.2. European Water Regulators (WAREG) scope of regulatory action and independence 87
Box 3.3. Developing effective coordination following the OECD Principles on Water Governance 89
Box 3.4. ESCOSA Business Model 94
Box 3.5. Ethical Based Regulation at WICS, UK 94
Box 3.6. Regionalisation in Italy: ARERA case study on territorial aggregation by uniform catchment areas 97
Box 3.7. Lessons from ARERA about increasing private sector investment 100

Follow OECD Publications on:

 http://twitter.com/OECD_Pubs

 http://www.facebook.com/OECDPublications

 http://www.linkedin.com/groups/OECD-Publications-4645871

▶ http://www.youtube.com/oecdilibrary

 http://www.oecd.org/oecddirect/

Executive summary

The increased frequency and intensity of water-related events in Brazil due to climate change puts people at risk, reduces the reliability of water infrastructure and undermines national food and energy security. In 2020, 1.1 million people were affected by floods and about 15 million by droughts, with many more affected by knock-on effects, such as higher food prices. In addition, the depletion in hydropower reservoirs that had started in 2013, meant that, in 2021, 213 million people, reliant on hydropower for two-thirds of their electricity, were at increased risk of electricity supply default. Urgent policy responses for water resilience are therefore needed to tackle the consequences of climate uncertainties.

The economic crisis following the COVID-19 pandemic has put additional strain on the capacity of Brazil to implement water resources and sanitation policies and reduce infrastructure gaps. Although, the Brazilian economy began to recover in 2021 (with projected growth of 5.2%), it was hit hard by COVID-19, contracting by 4.4%, above the world average (-3.4%) in 2020. The pandemic also exacerbated longstanding public health challenges. The pandemic also exacerbated longstanding public health challenges. Indeed, as of January 2022, Brazil had 2 899 per 1 million of COVID-19 related deaths ranking second in the Latin American and Caribbean (LAC) region. More than 100 million people in Brazil lack access to safe sanitation, while 21.6 million use inadequate sanitation facilities. Another 2.3 million people use unsafe water sources for human consumption and hygiene, while around 15 million urban dwellers lack access to safe drinking water and in in rural areas, around 8 million inhabitants lack access to safely managed water.

Brazil has adopted various funding and regulatory mechanisms to respond to water security challenges. In 2019, the National Water Security Plan (PNSH) set out an investment plan based on 114 actions to be taken by 2035, which should benefit one third of the 74 million people living in areas where water supply is at risk, and who will likely suffer from the consequential loss of industrial and agricultural production if no action is taken. The Water Security Programme (PSH) attached to the PNSH foresees a total of BRL 27.6 billion in capital investment and BRL 1.2 billion per year on average to operate and maintain water infrastructure. This doubles current levels (BLR 12.94 billion per year from 2013 to 2017 and BLR 13.7 billion in 2020, roughly 0.2% of GDP), although investments in the sanitation sector remain lower than in other sectors, such as electricity (0.54% of GDP in 2017). The 2020 Sanitation Law set conditions for legal clarity and transparency to engage the private sector in water-related infrastructure projects with the aim of building and maintaining sanitation services throughout the country. In doing so, the law expands ANA's role from managing water resources to defining standards for water sanitation services.

This report provides a series of policy recommendations and tailored action plan (Annex B) for Brazil to move from strategy to action in three main areas:

First, shift from a risk-based approach to a resilience approach to deal with future uncertainties due to climate change effects:

- Create a culture where water is regarded as a scarce and valuable resource, for instance through techniques such as the use of tariffs on a geographic (scarcity) basis. Issues to be taken into account include: the degree of water scarcity; the level of environmental sensitivity and degree of ecosystem stress; the proportion of used water that is returned to a location where it could be reused; and effluent quality. It is also key to identify how to safeguard low-income and vulnerable households and other users, such as through cross-subsidies, social tariffs, income support or special rebates or discounts. A culture of water can be also created through the introduction of more water-efficient fixtures, coupled with education and awareness-raising.

- Use incremental and scalable options for better managing water demand and supply, through fostering rational use and behavioural change, while also adopting a range of supply-side options in a timely manner.
- Leverage green infrastructure as flexible and cost-effective alternatives to hard engineering solutions to the water security challenge when possible, while generating beneficial outcomes for water quality, ecosystems, flood risk management and river flows.

Second, make river basin organisations deliver and use economic instruments to tackle water risks:

- Implement a multi-level governance system that ensures water management at the basin scale in coordination with state agencies and the federal government. This also implies evaluating whether catchment-based institutions are delivering on their mandate to identify possible governance gaps and plan measures to overcome them.
- Engage stakeholders in water resource management to ensure a balanced and representative consultation process that takes diverse ideas and opinions into account, and pay specific attention to the involvement of municipalities and the underserved/disadvantaged communities.
- Allocate water where it is most needed and attribute a value to water through economic instruments such as abstraction charges. These create incentives to reduce water demand and allocate water cost effectively while raising funds to finance infrastructure and integrated water resource management. Pragmatically, the initial priority could be to target users with the largest water withdrawals. To be more cost-effective, charges should be combined with other instruments such as water allocation regimes and minimum ecological river flows (direct regulation) and the promotion of best available technologies (information measures).

Third, accompany infrastructure development with regulatory oversight and monitoring. For this to happen, ANA, which is at the centre of the reform in the new Sanitation Law, would need to:

- Set up effective coordination mechanisms with sub-national authorities to ensure that the application of the new law creates no formal or perceived conflict across levels of government in relation to taking decisions, evaluating impacts and regularly reviewing implementation.
- Strengthen stakeholder engagement mechanisms to enhance the understanding of and compliance with the rules and regulations, and raise awareness of the activities of the regulator to increase public acceptance.
- Build adequate capacity and power for the regulator so that ANA's new mandate is accompanied by a focused effort to ensure adequate funding, skills and competences.

1 Governing water infrastructure for greater resilience

Worldwide, infrastructure plays a key role in responding to the pressures on water resources and enhancing water security. Those pressures will continue to increase in the coming decades because of demographic change, economic growth, pollution, land-use change, ecosystem degradation, and climate change. Brazil is no exception. The country made good progress in identifying and addressing challenges, funding and maintaining infrastructure based on public investment. However, the funding model has reached a limit, while technical skills and capacity, and stakeholder engagement need to be improved to further progress and move from a risk to a resilient approach. This chapter offers options to achieve these goals.

Infrastructure for water security in Brazil

The increased frequency and intensity of extreme, water-related events in Brazil due to climate change put people at risk, reduce the reliability of water infrastructure and have consequences for food and energy security. In 2020, 1.1 million people were affected by floods and about 15 million by droughts (ANA, 2021[1]). In 2021, the depletion in hydropower reservoirs due to a sequence of below-average hydrologic years starting in 2013 threatened the electricity supply for 213 million people who rely on hydropower for two-thirds of their electricity. Floods and droughts can simultaneously occur in different parts of the country, impacting the reliability of water infrastructure. For example, during droughts, reduced water inflow increases the uncertainties of reservoir storage, while the reduced capacity of multipurpose hydropower dams can generate tensions between users.

Rapid population growth and urbanisation in Brazil affect water infrastructure development. However, gaps remain, especially between urban and rural areas. In 1970, 51 million of the 93 million inhabitants lived in urban areas. By 2010, out of 190 million people, 160 million lived in urban centres or near the coast (IBGE, 2015[2]; ECLAC, 2012[3]). Due to population growth, by 2040, water demand is expected to grow by 43.5% compared to 2017, representing an increase of 4 337 billion m³ (Trata Brasil, 2020[4]). About 15 million Brazilians living in urban areas do not have access to safe drinking water protected from external contamination and available at home (Siwi/Unicef/World Bank, 2020[5]). In rural areas, 30% of the population (7.8 million inhabitants) lack access to safely managed water (WHO/UNICEF, 2021[6]). Untreated sewage reduced 13% in 10 years, from 62.2% in 2010, to 59.2% in 2014 and 49,2% in 2020, but remain high (MDR, 2020[7]). Other issues are related to water pollution. High BOD concentrations are found in rivers crossing large urban centres, which receive large organic pollution loads from untreated effluents and diffuse pollution (ANA, 2021[8]).

Overall, 95.2 million people lack proper sanitation services (MDR, 2020[7]). A total of 21.6 million uses inadequate sanitation facilities, while 2.3 million uses unsafe water sources for human consumption and personal and domestic hygiene. The lack of access is especially acute in indigenous villages and in urban peripheries, informal settlements and slums, where approximately 13 million Brazilians live. According to the Atlas Aguas – Water Security for Urban Water Supply, BRL 110.3 billion investment in water production, distribution and infrastructure replacement will be needed in 5570 urban centres by 2035 (ANA, 2021[8]).

The National Water Security Plan (PNSH) set out strategic infrastructure requirements in 2019 and an investment plan to 2035. Projects proposed in the PNSH will benefit one third of the 74 million people who live in areas where water supplies are at risk and where an economic impact of BRL 518 billion is likely to occur from loss of industrial and agricultural production in the absence of action. According to PNSH, there is a need for BRL 26.9 billion in investments in new, strategic water infrastructure by 2035, mainly to provide expansion of water storage and supply, of which BRL 17.6 billion by public federal funds (to date, BRL 13.2 billion have been already invested) (ANA/MDR, 2019[9]). Thus, alternative funding is needed to provide part of the strategic water infrastructure (ANA, 2019[10]). The Ministry of Regional Development (MDR) will monitor and update the PSH and proactively guide its implementation where necessary. In doing so, it will work with federal agencies, state institutions and other stakeholders to ensure that the programme ties in with others for the provision of sanitation and for the promotion of regional development. At each stage of each project, the ANA will provide a water infrastructure assessment certificate (CERTOH) to allow it to continue operating according to the quality standards (ANA, 2021[8]).

Investments needs are estimated to be almost double than the current peace. From 2013 to 2017, Brazil invested BLR 12.94 billion per year on water and sanitation (MRD, 2019[11])). In 2020, that amount reached BLR 13.7 billion. However, there is a need for BRL 357 billion in order to reach universal access to water and sanitation, which corresponds to BRL 23.8 Billion per year by 2033 (1.8 times the average investment currently observed). Other studies estimate the investment needed is BRL 498 billion, not counting BRL 255 billion due to asset depreciation, providing a total of BRL 753 billion (KPMG/ABICON, 2020[12]) or BRL

50.2 billion per year by 2033 (3.9 times the current investment rate). The new regulatory framework intends to attract more private investments in order to face that investment demand.

A modern approach to water security cannot rely only on infrastructure as such. It requires bottom-up regional development strategies to address economic and social disparities. The OECD (2015[13]) highlighted the need to overcome the legacy of a Keynesian approach in Brazil's public policy, based on intense public investment for the construction of large infrastructure. As such, measures towards greater water security (e.g., combining supply and demand, grey and green infrastructure, risk management and resilience, with a holistic view in connection with the environment, territorial development and land use) will entail robust water governance, as highlighted by the OECD Principles on Water Governance (Box 1.1).

> **Box 1.1. The OECD Principles on Water Governance**
>
> The OECD Principles on Water Governance aim to enhance water governance systems to manage "too much, too little and too polluted" water and foster universal access to drinking water and sanitation in a sustainable, integrated and inclusive way, at an acceptable cost and in a reasonable timeframe. The principles acknowledge that good governance is a means to master complexity and manage trade-offs in a policy domain that is sensitive to fragmentation, silos, scale mismatch, negative externalities, monopolies and capital-intensive investment. The principles consider good governance as helping solve water challenges using a combination of bottom-up and top-down processes while fostering constructive state-society relations. Bad governance, on the other hand, generates undue transaction costs and does not respond to place-based needs.
>
> The principles support effective, efficient and inclusive water governance systems:
>
> 1. Effectiveness relates to the contribution of governance to define clear sustainable water policy goals and targets at all levels of government, to implement those policy goals, and to meet expected targets.
> 2. Efficiency relates to the contribution of governance to maximise the benefits of sustainable water management and welfare at the least cost to society.
> 3. Trust and engagement relate to the contribution of governance to building public confidence and ensuring the inclusiveness of stakeholders through democratic legitimacy and fairness for society at large.
>
> The 12 principles are:
>
> - **Principle 1.** Clearly allocate and distinguish roles and responsibilities for water policymaking, policy implementation, operational management and regulation, and foster coordination across these responsible authorities.
> - **Principle 2.** Manage water at the appropriate scale(s) within integrated basin governance systems to reflect local conditions, and foster coordination between the different scales.
> - **Principle 3.** Encourage policy coherence through effective cross-sectoral coordination, especially between policies for water and the environment, health, energy, agriculture, industry, spatial planning and land use.
> - **Principle 4.** Adapt the level of capacity of responsible authorities to the complexity of water challenges to be met, and to the set of competencies required to carry out their duties.
> - **Principle 5.** Produce, update and share timely, consistent, comparable and policy-relevant water and water-related data and information, and use it to guide, assess and improve water policy.

- **Principle 6.** Ensure that governance arrangements help mobilise water finance and allocate financial resources in an efficient, transparent and timely manner.
- **Principle 7.** Ensure that sound water management regulatory frameworks are effectively implemented and enforced in pursuit of the public interest.
- **Principle 8.** Promote the adoption and implementation of innovative water governance practices across responsible authorities, levels of government and relevant stakeholders.
- **Principle 9.** Mainstream integrity and transparency practices across water policies, water institutions and water governance frameworks for greater accountability and trust in decision-making.
- **Principle 10.** Promote stakeholder engagement for informed and outcome-oriented contributions to water policy design and implementation.
- **Principle 11.** Encourage water governance frameworks that help manage trade-offs across water users, rural and urban areas, and generations.
- **Principle 12.** Promote regular monitoring and evaluation of water policy and governance where appropriate, share the results with the public and make adjustments when needed.

Figure 1.1. OECD Principles on Water Governance

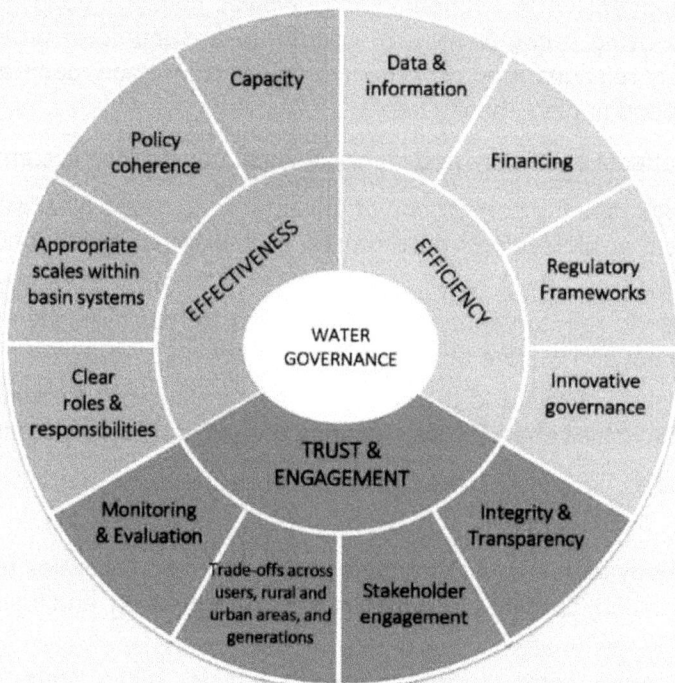

Source: OECD (2015[14]), *OECD Principles on Water Governance*, http://www.oecd.org/cfe/regional-policy/OECD-Principles-on-Water-Governance.pdf.

Getting the governance of water infrastructure right

Enhancing coordination across levels of government

Brazil has an institutional framework to plan and implement water infrastructure projects to enhance water security. In response to the need to develop water infrastructure, the National Water and Sanitation Agency (ANA) sits within the MDR, having moved from the Ministry of the Environment. In 2019, ANA published the PNSH (ANA, 2019[10]), focusing on two types of intervention: (1) multi-purpose dams for water supply and flood control, and (2) infrastructure to distribute and transfer water resources. Suggested solutions are based on a comprehensive evaluation and mapping of the water risks in the country using the Water Security Index (ISH), which combines human, economic, ecosystem and resilience criteria. The ISH revealed that coastal areas and the northeast part of the country are the most vulnerable.

Implementation of the PNSH will require coordination across levels of government. In Brazil, water resources management is a responsibility of the 27 states and the Federal District, and there is a history of participatory democracy based on more than 200 river basin committees. The OECD (2015[15]) recognised that Brazil's river basins are very diverse in terms of their hydrological characteristics and level of economic development, and in terms of institutional capacity and skills. Solutions to water management challenges need to reflect this diversity and the reality of dissimilar levels of progress towards overarching policy objectives. Moreover, potential tensions between federal and state priorities are exacerbated by challenges related to the "double dominion" over water management, whereby competences over federal and state rivers are allocated to different levels of government.

As part of the appraisal of any major capital project proposal, **roles and responsibilities** must be in place for each stage, from the initial policy decision through to operation and maintenance of the infrastructure, as argued by the OECD Principles on Water Governance (OECD, 2015[13]). Options to consider include:

- **Strengthening the relationship between all relevant institutions**. The Ministry of Regional Development, to which ANA belongs, should have a central role in relation to water infrastructure, with the engagement of entities simultaneously relevant to water resources management and to the social and economic development of the country, such as the CODEVASF (Company for the Development of São Francisco and Parnaíba Valleys) and DNOCS (National Department of Infrastructure against Droughts), both linked to the Ministry of Regional Development (Ministry of Regional Development, 2021[16]; 2021[17]).
- **Formalising institutional arrangements for decision making** about every major infrastructure project to ensure that roles, responsibilities and funding are clear and in place at each stage of development.
- **Setting a legislative basis for green infrastructure and cross-sector strategic engagement**. The extent of the policy ambition for green infrastructure as a climate change adaptation measure needs to be agreed between relevant ministries. Planning, funding and delivering green infrastructure must be more formal, with legislative and budgetary support, and clear accountability for delivery depending on the nature of the scheme. An optimised portfolio of grey and green infrastructure[1] appears critical to build and sustain water security and resilience. For example, nature-based solutions are among the most efficient to sustainably increase water yields (Box 1.2).

Box 1.2. Reaping the benefits of green infrastructure in the water sector

Green infrastructure is defined as "a strategically planned network of natural and semi-natural areas with other environmental features designed and managed to deliver a wide range of ecosystem services. It incorporates green spaces (or blue if aquatic ecosystems are concerned) and other physical features in terrestrial (including coastal) and marine areas" (EC, 2013[18]). Green infrastructure is recognised as part of the answer to water challenges in OECD countries, especially when cities compete with other users (e.g., agriculture and thermal energy) for the water they need, and when water management is addressed in relation to land use and other policies.

The United Nations Environment Programme (2014[19]) lists green infrastructures for water resource management, some of which are useful in an urban context. Colin Green (OECD, 2013[20]) adds demand management and local processing of black or grey water to this list. Technologies related to sludge recycling, wastewater-energy generation and water cycle energy efficiency could also be considered. Green infrastructure provides solutions to all four risks that determine urban water security: droughts, floods, pollution and ecosystem resilience. Furthermore, it must be noted that most of the technologies inventoried in Table 1.1 are mature. Some have been in use for centuries. For example, Venice has relied on rainwater harvesting since its infancy, while Paris adopted a three-pipe system in the 19th Century, supplying non-potable water to uses that did not require potable water.

The benefits of green infrastructures are well-documented. The Nature Conservancy (McDonald and Shemie, 2014[21]) computes that if cities invested in watershed conservation, 700 million people could receive better-quality water, and water utilities could save USD 890 million a year in water treatment costs. Watershed conservation may be particularly relevant to low-income cities that cannot afford the capital and operation and maintenance (O&M) costs of built infrastructures.

Table 1.1. Green Infrastructure solutions for water resource management

	Urban water management issue							
	Water supply and sanitation (including drought)	Water quality regulation			Moderation of extreme events (floods)			Protection of ecosystems
		Water purification	Biological control	Water temperature control	Riverine flood control	Urban stormwater runoff	Coastal flood (storm) control	
	Green infrastructure solution							
Demand management	X							X
Local processing of black or grey water	X	X	X					
Wetlands restoration/conservation	X	X	X	X	X			X
Constructing wetlands	X	X	X	X	X			X
Water harvesting						X		
Green spaces	X	X		X		X		X
Permeable pavements	X	X				X		X
Green roofs						X		X
Protecting/restoring mangroves, coastal marshes, dunes, reefs							X	X

	Corresponding grey infrastructure (primary service level)					
Dams, groundwater pumping	X			X		
Dams, levees				X	X	
Water distribution systems	X					
Water treatment plants		X	X			
Urban stormwater infrastructure						X
Sea walls						X

Green infrastructure can be significantly more cost-effective than grey solutions. However, it usually must co-exist and interact with grey infrastructure. The key to successful implementation is land planning, ideally at a basin scale, since, although rainfall cannot be altered, how it runs off land depends on land strategies and landscape modifications.

Green infrastructure can provide multi-functional benefits. For example, urban parks and other green spaces in La Marjal de Alicante, Spain, provide multi-functional amenities, which are an attractive alternative to conventionally engineered flood defences. Such schemes are in use in many countries, using combinations of bypass tunnels, natural or artificial bypass channels, or large scale reconnection of the flood plain with the river to restore it to its natural purpose.

Source: Adapted from UNEP (2014[19]), *Green Infrastructure Guide for Water Management: Ecosystem-based Management Approaches for Water-related Infrastructure Projects*, United Nations Environment Programme; OECD (2013[20]), "Barriers to and Incentives for the Adoption of Green Water Infrastructure", OECD, Paris; OECD (2015[22]), *Water and Cities: Ensuring Sustainable Futures*, http://dx.doi.org/10.1787/9789264230149-en; McDonald, R. and D. Shemie (2014[21]), *Urban Water Blueprint: Mapping Conservation Solutions to the Global Water Challenge*, https://www.nature.org/content/dam/tnc/nature/en/documents/Urban_Water_Blueprint.pdf; EC (2013[18]), *Building a Green Infrastrcuture for Europe*, European Commission, https://ec.europa.eu/environment/nature/ecosystems/docs/green_infrastructure_broc.pdf;

Aiming for resilience

Under the principle of subsidiarity, Brazilian legislation indicates the division of tasks between national, state and river basin plans, which often lack effective implementation. The State should focus on strategic issues and larger scales, and address strategic issues in their regional contexts, while river basin plans, with a more local approach, should focus on executive and operational tasks. According to Article 35, of the 1997 Water Law, the National Water Resources Council (CNRH) promotes the coordination of water resource plans with national, regional, state and sectoral plans, and approves the National Water Plan, making sure its targets are met. However, the National Water Resources Plan is too broad to set specific priorities and fails to link to broader development strategies. River and state basin plans are often "paper tigers", not implemented due to a lack of buy-in from the stakeholders and decision makers within whose remit measures might have to be taken and funds allocated. Plans often lack proper implementation (OECD, 2015[15]).

Resilience thinking can develop more robust plans and flexible solutions. Resilience is not simply whether a system would be able to maintain supplies in the event of a drought, but also how it might respond to a range of shocks such as loss of power on a wide scale or cyber-attacks. Climate change creates a range of potential impacts that infrastructure will need to be resilient against. For example, dams will need to cope with changing flow levels, and urban surface-water drainage systems will need to cope with higher runoff rates compared to the historic record. Infrastructure adjacent to rivers, such as drinking water and wastewater treatment plants are likely to face an increasing risk of inundation.

System resilience is a critical part of the User Pays Principle, which aims for equitable sharing of costs and access to a resource, coupled with efficient supply of water and resource conservation through demand management. A 'presumption of change' is key to assumptions around levels of resilience and to identifying the conditions for recovery from failure. Institutional and governance arrangements are also integral to resilience. The economic regulator in England and Wales, Ofwat, has a legal duty to secure the resilience of the water companies it regulates through their planning and investment, including for operation and maintenance (O&M), and to ensure that they are managing water sustainably and increasing the efficiency of use by their customers. All companies' quinquennial business plans are required to address resilience, such as by good design, not relying on single assets of a specific type, greater connectivity in their networks, protecting their assets as far as possible, and improving their incident response processes so that when there is a failure it can be identified and dealt with quickly, and before it has the potential to cause consequential failures.

To respond to the increasing risk of droughts, new infrastructure planning should consider:

- **Including worst-case scenarios** for the potential impact of climate change and levels of future water demand. ANA made progress in understanding and managing risks to water supplies, and this approach now needs to include resilience thinking so that the duration and magnitude of failures is minimised. This assessment should then inform water planning, along the lines of 'hoping for the best but planning for the worst. This will help identify capacity gaps and technical skills to be addressed and prioritise spending.

- **Assessing system vulnerabilities** to shocks such as more extreme droughts than those planned for, or from cyber-attacks and telemetry failures. Also, consider measures implemented to mitigate impacts.

- **Ensuring greater reliability and resilience** of existing supply systems, and introducing a wider range of source types less vulnerable to drought. For example, in Spain, increasing uncertainty over the reliability of abstractions led to greater reliance on less conventional sources of water than dams. The country has 765 desalination plants with an output of over 100m³ per day, producing around five million m³ per day, for urban supply, agriculture and industry. Desalinated water can be more expensive than resources from dams and rivers, depending on how externalities are considered, and produces large volumes of brine to be disposed of. Water reuse is also important in Spain, with 368 plants in operation or planned, yielding nearly 11% of the total available water. There are strict rules and quality standards for each type of use. Some uses are prohibited, such as for human supply, the food industry, hospitals, mollusc aquaculture etc. The EU is considering what standards to apply across Europe to address real and perceived concerns about risks to public health.

- **Developing drought management plans** for new and existing assets. It is important to develop drought management plans that set out accountabilities and actions agreed in advance with stakeholders across all sectors. Plans would help manage demand, with defined triggers for each step as drought intensifies. Where emergency resources can be utilised, it is important to agree on the conditions for their use and any mitigation measures to offset environmental and social impacts. Drought management plans contribute to moving from crisis management to risk management, as they require risk assessments, monitoring, and clear decision-making based on a series of indicators.

Ensuring policy coherence

Water security is a long-term policy requiring costly infrastructure that will last for 50 years or more. It has cross-sectoral policy impacts at national, regional and local level. Fundamental synergies can be found between water and environment, territorial policies and land use. First, conservation of water ecosystems should be enhanced to guarantee water for all necessary uses in the long term. Second, high urbanisation rates in Brazil highlight the need for compatibility with territorial development policies, with consequences for water resource management. Third, land use directly affects the magnitude of extreme, water-related events, such as floods, especially for vulnerable people. As such, coordination across policy areas and sectors is essential so that water infrastructure contributes to wider development goals. This integrated view can be achieved by:

- **Initiating cross-departmental dialogues** between ministries, such as establishing a permanent commission for policy integration to enhance cross-sectoral coherence and identify multiple benefits from every policy decision which could impact water directly or indirectly. It is not always recognised that water plans such as the PNSH generate wider consequences that might benefit or adversely impact parts of society, or stimulate or stifle economic growth in different areas. A permanent commission for integrated planning would ensure that the impact of plans on each other is considered explicitly, and synergies, gaps and adverse impacts identified. Embedding this approach would deliver more efficient investment, improve coordination between fragmented institutions and ensure that the multiplicity of plans focuses on delivering positive outcomes.
- **Extending the concept of integrated work into routine practice**. There is currently no institutional model to deliver an integrated approach to planning horizontally across different ministries and vertically between layers of government in order to overcome the fragmented approach and lack of clear accountability. Each level of government needs to have clear accountability for communicating and delivering on its role.
- **Taking into account the implications of wider policy decisions** for water supply and sanitation, and taking proactive measures at an early stage in the planning process so that water becomes an enabler rather than a hurdle. Policy and legislation for municipal developments should consider water impacts, with developers and development authorities accountable for funding the additional demand they put on water infrastructure and ensuring that construction meets standards for water efficiency and minimising surface water runoff. Economic instruments may have a part in ensuring that development is properly controlled and in accordance with agreed rules; enforcement of the rules and penalties may be needed where these are ignored.
- **Making a policy decision on levels of service** for public water supply and other key sectors (i.e., an acceptable frequency of failure, such as during a once-a-century drought), and to confirm sectoral priorities during water emergencies, besides those already set by Law No. 9.433/1997, changed by Law No.14.026. Water supply planning in Brazil is based on the worst drought recorded in the hydrological record, but this fails to recognise that the worst drought to stress supply systems will not have happened yet. Conflicts between users during times of water stress are likely to increase unless action is taken to manage them. Making a policy decision on levels of service must be based on inclusive discussions that involve both public water supply and other key sectors, and must confirm sectoral priorities during water emergencies.

Building capacities

OECD (2015[15]) shows that Brazilian states have different capacity needs and priorities towards water resources management. Problems can relate to understaffing and underfunding, lack of proper enforcement and compliance with the law, and incomplete water information systems. Especially at the state level, decisions should be enforced and plans elaborated with the participation of users and civil society. Greater empowerment and qualification of state water agencies can help achieve this, making those agencies fully accountable for the implementation of all decisions. This emphasis on states should not exclude the role of the river basin committees and agencies but drive a learning curve whereby states, as they become stronger, will likely contribute to strengthening river basin institutions as well. In practice, action is needed on two fronts for stronger state authorities in water resources management: at technical and financial levels.

For new water infrastructure, it is important that state and municipal actors have adequate capacity for planning and implementation. This implies:

- **Addressing technical capacity** through structured training programmes at an appropriate scale to ensure the operation and maintenance of sophisticated water supply systems and treatment processes. Technical capacities at municipal and state levels could be developed or strengthened to assess the effectiveness and efficiency of wastewater treatment and drinking water delivery against international standards for drinking water quality and pollution limits, and benchmark costs with other countries.
- **Piloting different approaches** to skills development to ensure consistent professional standards across the country.
- **Developing training courses for river basin committee members** to help them understand the complexities of water management and the trade-offs involved in decisions. For example, where there are large numbers of stakeholders in a particular sector, such as irrigators, the training could help make it clear that a user association would be able to speak for them and have more influence on decision-making.
- **Setting up mechanisms to share best practices** within and between states, together with structured programmes for the continued professional development of staff. This could be done through virtual networks and discussion fora for specialists in particular disciplines, or periodic conferences or workshops to present case studies and encourage peer-to-peer learning.
- **Considering how professional institutions** could assess and recognise competence, and support continued professional development.
- **Considering the benefits from the amalgamation** of delivery bodies (as happens extensively in Europe) to provide efficiencies through economies of scale and adoption of best practices. Municipalities, particularly smaller ones, are vulnerable when technical skills are offered by just a few individuals, so sharing resources and amalgamating training can increase resilience (Box 1.3).

> **Box 1.3. Enhancing capacity at a sub-national level in the EU**
>
> The 28 states within the European Union are, to a degree, analogous to Brazil, with issues relating to different levels of capacity to manage water infrastructure. Standards are set centrally for a wide range of water-related criteria such as drinking water quality, bathing water quality, wastewater treatment and the ecological status of rivers. Member States have different levels of compliance; their performance is related to their capacity and capability, and the funds available to invest in improvements. Treated drinking water reaches 96% of the population (2015 figures), but the management of sewage effluent is more variable. The coverage of sewer networks reaches 92%, but only 82% is sent for treatment.
>
> As the EU progressed its rollout of standards on wastewater treatment, it became clear that responsibility for this activity in most countries lies with municipalities, which have neither the capacity nor the technical skills to deliver it effectively. Actions to enhance capacity have included:
>
> - **Appropriate scale:** In many countries, there was consolidation across municipalities to achieve critical mass and economies of scale. France consolidated the work of 35,000 municipalities into 1,200 to deliver these efficiencies. Denmark took a similar route in 2008, reducing from 1,350 municipalities to 98. Where sewage treatment is privatised, it there must be independent regulation; otherwise the contractor enjoys the benefits while the client carries the risk.
> - **Financial support:** The EU provides financial support where needed, and imposes sanctions – infraction proceedings – where performance is poor and commitment for improvements lacking. The use of conditionalities to fund schemes proposed at a state or municipal level has

> increased compliance with regulatory standards. The combination of carrots and sticks has proved very effective in delivering significant improvements in access to water and sanitation, and to protecting and improving the water environment throughout Europe.

Source: OECD/ANA (2019-21[23]), "Water Governance Workshops".

Improving data collection and analysis

Forecasting demand and developing options are the foundation of water security planning. However, assumptions about population growth, urbanisation, water use in homes and industry, and irrigation demand are all subject to considerable uncertainty. Understanding the impact of uncertainties in forecasts is essential to developing a robust and adaptable plan that delivers cost-effective solutions, and which manages the risk of supply failure. Moreover, the relevant information does not lie exclusively with one level of government, and actors depend on each other's knowledge to disseminate information between relevant levels of government. In practice, according to (OECD, 2015[15]), sub-national governments tend to have more information than national ones about local needs and preferences, and about the implementation and costs of local policies. Unless they generate and publish this information on a timely basis and communicate it to the central level, an information gap can occur. Nevertheless, the sub-national level's views are only "partial" – limited to a specific area or territory. Thus, the central government plays an indispensable role in managing the information to support a broader vision of public policy objectives. Information can also be used to identify capacity needs. Once again, this indicates a relationship of mutual dependence. To improve data collection and analysis, efforts should include:

- **Producing and collecting good data** for managing water and assessing the potential of different options beyond grey infrastructure. Water security planning requires a broad range of data across different disciplines, such as hydrology, ecology, demographics and social science. It is essential to review the data needs for water supply security planning and establish the mechanisms to collect and store it so that it is accessible for use within a water planning process that takes account of climate change and adopts a twin track approach: implementing demand management measures in tandem with cultivating resource options.
- **Improving data on water demand** beyond historic data that has been used for planning purposes. There is a need for more and better data on water demand to improve models for forecasting. Data should be objective driven. In other words, they need to be collected for a purpose, which will help to ensure quality and consistency.
- **Integrating data collection and planning processes** with a clear overall purpose. Long-tern planning (10-yearly with a 30-year horizon) already exists within the power sector and could be a model for water, which would also need to ensure that it is integrated with national development strategies. Having a single entity to oversee it could be beneficial.
- **Using scenarios** can help understand risk and uncertainty, and what contingencies might be needed if reality deviates significantly from the plan. The PNSH only extends to 2035 and uses historic rainfall and flow records as the basis to develop schemes. The dams and transfers constructed will have asset lives well past that date and, by not taking account of climate change, there is a risk that the yield characteristics of the sources will alter significantly, jeopardising the benefits of the scheme and the options chosen. The PNSH should be tested for risk, resilience and uncertainties using scenarios for different levels of demand and for water availability under climate change on timescales that are compatible with the expected life of water infrastructure.

- **Performing cost-benefit analysis** of the performance of infrastructure should be carried out to define if remedial works are needed, or whether low-cost improvements such as better control systems would allow it to perform better. The cost-benefit assessment for a new scheme should therefore consider a 'Do Nothing' option to see whether the capital and associated operational costs for O&M are more cost-effective and sustainable when the money is spent on improving and maintaining existing infrastructure, or on managing demand so as to negate the need for additional infrastructure.

Funding the multi-purpose operation and maintenance of water infrastructure

Brazil prioritises funding and spending for new infrastructure over O&M. The PSH indicates that the BRL 27.58 billion of new investment would require an average annual operation and maintenance spend of BRL 1.2 billion. It is just as important to maintain existing assets so that they perform as intended and risks are minimised. An example is the maintenance of 1454 dams assessed at high risk by the ANA Dam Safety Report (ANA, 2021[24]). The report presented 21 953 dams with volume information, many of which are at high risk of failure. There are thousands (3 355 multi-purpose dams) of small (less than one hectometre^3) private dams and around 400 large (more than 10 hectometre^3) public dams. Among the public dams, 281 belong to the Federal Government. A total of 3 690 dams are classified as high hazard, with the potential for loss of life if they failed, while 1161 dams are simultaneously classified as high hazard and high risk. Issues revealed by the report include spillway deterioration, concrete failure, leakage, piping and slope failure. Large irrigation infrastructure such as concrete canals is also deteriorating. These dams have now been prioritised for funding, but public funds have proved to be highly variable year-on-year, making planning for remediation and ongoing maintenance very problematic. Even where funding has been budgeted, actual expenditure reached 42% of the available sum. In 2020, BRL 162 million were budget for dam safety interventions, and BRL 58 million were actually spent, including federal and state budgets.

Better O&M may prove to be a more cost-effective option than new infrastructure. The cost of maintenance is specific to each asset, and will depend on a range of parameters such as what it is (e.g. dam, pump, pipeline etc.), its age, the materials used in its construction etc. The cost tends to be viewed in isolation, and not considered against the cost of failure. Routine inspection and preventative maintenance can help avoid such costly failures, and is an expense, which should be assessed as part of the approvals process for any new infrastructure. Apart from funding by the government or dam owners and operators (most dams are operated by DNOCS and CODEVASF), other options for O&M include payment from beneficiaries or new sources such as recreation or renewable energy generation. As yet, there is no experience of developing different funding models and it is questionable how realistic this would be for the foreseeable future. Box 1.4 provides an overview of funds applied in the European Union.

There is almost no culture among users of water services of having to pay for the benefit they receive from the associated infrastructure. Even where charges are levied for water use, it is not clear whether these should be spent on O&M or on new assets. The result is progressive underinvestment in maintenance and a deterioration in asset condition, which is likely to negate the benefit of the new infrastructure. More often, because dams are typically a long distance from the population served, their remoteness results in a lack of awareness of the true cost of the service or any willingness to pay for it. One exception is in Arroio Duro in Rio Grande do Sul, where users took over the operation of a reservoir, which benefits local communities and farmers, and charge a fee to users to cover the operating costs. Innovative funding options have also been explored, such as the development of floating solar energy generation, which may have potential because it creates an additional funding source for the O&M of dams. It is proposed that the successful bidder for the right to install floating solar systems would be expected to assume responsibility for the O&M of the dam. The incentive for investment in this model depends on the conditions established in the bid, particularly if there is a legacy of underspend and the asset condition is problematic.

OECD (2017[25]) looked at how water charges could contribute to current and long-term policy objectives, and deliver results for improving water management. The report set out a case for change, identified challenges to implementation and set out a way forward. A critical finding was that water charges must operate within an effective, enforced regulatory regime for abstractions and discharges; without these in place pollution, wasteful use and misallocation will hinder economic growth and improvements in social welfare. Water charges must be defined and used in conjunction with other policy instruments, such as water allocation regimes and water quality goals. Well-designed charges can influence behaviour, but must be applied within a clear regulatory, monitoring and enforcement regime. Charge payers need to understand what the money is being used for and how they will benefit from the expenditure; setting them at a level which is likely to deliver policy objectives is a challenge in Brazil. A major problem is that the capital investments planned in Brazil will require financial resources far greater than the potential revenue from water charges, which cannot legally be used to fund operations.

A more structured and explicit approach to funding for O&M from different budget streams is needed, as is application of charges to beneficiaries, allocation of sufficient funds for the routine maintenance of infrastructure, and institutional capacity development. In practice, a functioning model for funding and maintaining water infrastructure in the context of more integrated and coordinated public policies could be achieved by:

- **Clarifying responsibility for O&M,** transferring it to state governments, as is not currently the case, and increasing stakeholder involvement.
- **Applying preventative maintenance** so that assets function more reliably and are cheaper in the long run than assets that have not been properly maintained and fail repeatedly or catastrophically. Implementing a programme of routine preventative maintenance for water supply and wastewater assets would help ensure that they can reliably deliver target levels of service to customers.
- **Conditioning the availability of federal funding** for state and municipal priorities on regulatory compliance and the effective operation and maintenance of water infrastructure.
- **Exploring other mechanisms for funding,** including use of the Land Tax as a mechanism for funding some water infrastructure, such as for flood risk management, and the potential for developers to help fund the consequent water impacts. There is a risk that funding water infrastructure is viewed as the responsibility of one government department or ministry. However, the constructed assets may provide a much wider benefit. As such, a more structured and explicit approach to funding the development and maintenance of water infrastructure from different budget streams may be justified. For example, the proportion of the capital and revenue costs of a resource that provides benefit to energy or agriculture could be funded by the relevant ministry. In addition, applying charges to the ultimate beneficiaries can provide a reliable revenue stream. Funding of multi-beneficiary structures would depend on finding a process by which all beneficiaries are able to pay their share. Although agriculture is cited as a sector, which could struggle to afford to pay, it is important to distinguish between large-scale, export-oriented agriculture and subsistence farmers; there may need to be separate charging regimes to reflect affordability. The way in which agricultural subsidies are targeted should be reviewed as part of this process. Municipalities are required to charge a Land Tax, but few do, even though this could be a source of revenue for flood prevention measures or drought supply security.
- **Applying different tariff structures** on a sectoral or geographic (scarcity) basis. In this case, some issues to be taken into account are: the degree of water scarcity; the level of environmental sensitivity and degree of ecosystem stress; the proportion of used water that returned to a location where it could be reused; and effluent quality. It is also key to identify how to safeguard low-income and vulnerable households and other users, such as through cross-subsidies, social tariffs, income support or special rebates or discounts. There is a question of whether, in a period of economic recovery, it is feasible for funds for the sustainable operation and maintenance of water infrastructure to be provided by the central government or whether users should be required to pay

according to the benefit they derive in order to fully fund the O&M. Taking the analogy of the central cohesion fund in Europe, to support poorer states, there may be a case for the equivalent in Brazil, in the same way that individual users who cannot afford their bill would be subsidised by others. Cross-subsidies can create greater equity, but also can create tensions – as can the divide between rich and poor.

- **Agreeing on restriction rules and compensation fund**: there is general agreement that Brazil needs to have plans in place before a crisis so that actions, accountabilities and desired outcomes are clear at each pre-determined stage of a drought, mitigation measures are established, and the rules for restricting use have been agreed. The process for doing so should be inclusive and have a formalised governance system. For example, this could include agreeing drought adaptation measures such as rules for restricting certain types of use as a drought progresses, potentially establishing a compensation fund using abstraction charges so that lower priority users are not financially disadvantaged if they are restricted during a drought. The process for doing so should be inclusive and have formalised governance to ensure that funds are ring-fenced and used for the intended purpose.

- **Setting up incentives and penalties** to ensure that infrastructure is properly maintained and operated. Droughts and supply failures have an economic and social cost for both urban citizens and agriculture, but this is difficult to quantify. There is a perception by some that previous droughts have affected some sectors unevenly (agriculture in particular) but there is little culture of preventative planning. Incentives and penalties may be needed.

- **Revising subsidies** is important to understand whether agricultural subsidies are leading to poor water management or unsustainable farming practice, which could have an adverse impact on water resources, such as from the use of fertilisers and biocides causing pollution. Extending the application of the Water Producer Programme across more river basins could be also considered.

- **Improving transparency** about the need for these decisions at the highest levels of government. The availability of funding will always be a constraint on the level of service ambition, but greater transparency on what is being provided could make it easier to move towards levels of charging that support O&M as well as new capital investment.

Box 1.4. Financial support for water infrastructure in the EU

Across the European Union, there is financial support for water infrastructure. Obtaining it requires that charges are in place for the management of water resources. However, in some countries this is not fully developed. Poorer Member States such as Romania and Bulgaria struggle to find the resources to invest in improving or developing infrastructure. Where this is the case, the EU can subsidise the activity to deliver improvements and ensure multi-level policy coherence in order to work towards reducing disparities between Member States with regards to GDP per capita. The so-called 'cohesion funding' of around EUR 63 billion can provide up to 85% of investment needed for the country to meet EU standards, such as on wastewater treatment. However, such funding is conditional on, among other criteria, there being coherent river basin management plans in place, which should include plans of action to deliver the identified improvements. There must also be tariffs in place. In other words, for a country to receive financial assistance, it must be seen to be doing as much as it can to achieve resilience within the constraints of its economy.

Source: OECD/ANA (2019-21[23]), "Water Governance Workshops".

Developing demand management

Demand management techniques such as education and raising awareness of opportunities to save water in homes and businesses are often lower-cost alternatives than developing large infrastructure. However, they require good data on water usage and effective communication with water users. Just as green infrastructure can provide more flexible and cost-effective alternatives to hard engineering solutions (Box 1.5), demand management can provide an alternative to dams and transfers. However, it can be challenging to persuade customers to be more careful with water use if losses from the distribution network are high. Reducing leakage not only makes more water available for supply, but also sends a signal that the supplier is serious about the need for water conservation. Developing demand management as an essential component of sustainable and resilient water supplies includes:

- **Understanding the actions** needed to manage demand in different sectors, such as industry and agriculture, and in the case of domestic water use.
- **Establishing mechanisms** to share resources equitably and efficiently. A good start would be to assess the potential benefits of different demand management techniques and develop a demand management strategy and communication programme to reach all sectors, with a delivery plan to implement the actions with the greatest potential without delay.
- **Creating a demand management culture** where water is regarded as a scarce and valuable resource. Techniques such as the use of tariffs or the introduction of more water-efficient fixtures, fittings and appliances, coupled with education and awareness-raising could all help create this culture. The application of tariffs could depend on the use, water scarcity or environmental impact, and there should be safeguards for those who would struggle to pay for an essential service.
- **Defining targets for water efficiency** to drive action. For this to be effective, however, there needs to be a coherent demand management and communications strategy in place, and agreed mechanisms for equitable allocation and charging.
- **Assessing the potential benefits of different demand management techniques** and developing a demand management strategy and communication programme to reach all sectors, with a delivery plan to implement the actions with greatest potential without delay. This should include a programme of leakage reduction with performance targets, benchmarked against international good practice together with programmes of awareness-raising to improve the efficiency of industrial and agricultural processes. Household demand management could also include education and awareness raising, the distribution of water efficient fixtures and fittings such as low-flow shower heads and cistern displacement devices, water efficiency labelling of appliances, and nudge messaging on bills. Regulatory penalties and incentives could be applied in the most water-scarce areas.

Box 1.5. International experience in moving from supply to demand management

- The **European Commission** has adopted demand management as a priority for water management, including efficiency measures and effective pricing policies. In addition to pricing, various techniques can be used to improve water efficiency in agriculture, such as changing crop patterns and planting dates, and improved irrigation systems. In distribution networks leakage rates are up to 50% of the system input volume, with the potential for significant savings. Another key challenge relates to land use and agricultural practices that threaten water quality and quantity, and a large proportion of the water quality failures across Europe results from poor agricultural practice. In 2012, the European Commission prepared a Blueprint to set out the water policy agenda. The Blueprint demonstrates the potential for preserving water resources and aquatic ecosystems, indicates how water availability could evolve and suggests

> tools to improve water allocation, such as ecosystem needs and water efficiency targets, to take account of uncertainties about future development, reducing risk and increasing ecosystem resilience. The Blueprint presents policy proposals and recommendations that set the EU water agenda, in particular under the Common Implementation Strategy (CIS) of the Water Framework Directive.
>
> - The region of **Murcia**, in southwest Spain, is informally known as "Europe's garden". One out of every ten agro-food products exported by Spain comes from this region; 21.4% of the wealth of the region and 28.4% of total employment depend directly and indirectly on the agri-food sector. This area is very active for agricultural production despite its location in a traditionally water-stressed area. Most water used for irrigation purposes is groundwater (40.9% of total water resources used by the sector) and a significant portion of the surface water that is used originates in the Tajo-Segura transfer. The estimated water deficit to irrigate the entire agricultural area in the region is 143 hm³/year, rising to 303 hm³/year when accounting for the threshold of natural recharge of the aquifer. Without the Tajo-Segura transfer, both deficit figures increase to 276 hm³/year (27.7% of demand) and 436 hm³/year (43.7% of demand) respectively. Authorities and research institutions agree that political will is essential to ensure the sustainability of water resources in an economically viable manner while protecting the environment. In the region, good water culture has shaped the lifestyle and way of working, which has led to many efforts in collecting information and reflecting on sustainable demand management, managing incentives for water users and benefitting from technology to increase efficiency in water resources management.
>
> - The US state of **California** in recent years has endured the longest drought in its history, lasting 376 weeks beginning on 27 December 2011 and ending on 5 March 2019. However, while harvested acreage in California declined during the drought, agricultural revenue remained high due to a range of response strategies. Growers changed crops, improved their irrigation practices, fallowed land, engaged in water transfers, received insurance payments and pumped more groundwater. These strategies helped buffer the state's agricultural sector from drought-period losses and contributed to far fewer job losses than had been projected.
>
> With the mounting challenges related to climate change, urbanisation and demographic growth, responses may rely on policy coherence across different sectors, such as agriculture and food. For example local production and proximity, and a policy against food waste may have consequences for water quantity and quality. Certainly, impacts on jobs in relation to a different food policy (both internal and external/export) should be considered and offset. The question is how to decouple economic growth from environmental damage when the aim is to allow economic growth in the agricultural sector, which is responsible for 70% of water consumption globally but contributes little financially.
>
> Source: OECD (2021[26]), *Water Governance in Peru*, https://doi.org/10.1787/568847b5-en.

Engaging stakeholders

Investing in natural infrastructure can contribute to managing pollution risks as well as supporting low flows. However, showcasing the benefits of ecosystem services is important to raising awareness among stakeholders and encouraging them to participate. The use of ecosystem economic valuations as tested tools for analysis is increasing, so that decision makers can weigh the costs and benefits of alternative choices for water infrastructure. Moreover, if ecosystem valuations encourage relevant stakeholders to participate – such as water service providers, rural communities and agricultural users – then better informed and consensus-based decisions can be made. Enhancing stakeholder engagement for inclusive decision-making can be achieved through:

- **Greater participation by stakeholders in operational and investment decisions**, which might imply developing the capability of existing river basin committees. Where there are large numbers of stakeholders in one sector, such as irrigators, they are likely to have more influence on decision-making if they belong to a user association that is able to speak for them. In some areas it may be possible to move towards collaborative, cooperative user groups responsible for funding the operation and maintenance of infrastructure, and the monitoring of compliance with agreed rules. It was recognised that, in some states, if the river basin committees were to fulfil this role, there would be a lack of capacity and technical capability, and these would need to be developed. For dialogue to be effective there would also need to be clear sectoral policies to determine priorities and agree the level of funding and standard of service for each sector.
- **Stakeholder consultation and engagement on the regulation and management of each scheme**, with clearly identified roles and accountabilities. This will help ensure that changes in demand and water availability are managed sustainably and transparently. Over time, experience in the operation of a major water resources scheme will identify ways in which the operation and management can be improved and become more responsive to changes in demand from users or fluctuations in water availability. In addition, as users understand the regulatory framework, compliance should improve and create the potential for lighter touch regulation to take place.

References

ANA (2021), *Brazil Water Resources Conjuncture Report*, https://relatorio-conjuntura-ana-2021.webflow.io/ (accessed on 7 January 2022). [1]

ANA (2021), *Dam Safety Report 2021*, Agência Nacional de Águas, https://www.snisb.gov.br/relatorio-anual-de-seguranca-de-barragem/2021. [24]

ANA (2021), *Water Work Sustainability Assessment Certificate - CERTOH*, Agência Nacional de Águas, https://www.gov.br/ana/pt-br/assuntos/seguranca-hidrica/certoh (accessed on 15 December 2021). [8]

ANA (2019), *Plano Nacional de Segurança Hídrica*, Agência Nacional de Águas, https://pnsh.ana.gov.br/home. [10]

ANA/MDR (2019), *National Water Security Plan - PNSH*, https://pnsh.ana.gov.br/pdf/ingles.pdf. [9]

EC (2013), *Building a Green Infrastrcuture for Europe*, European Commission, https://ec.europa.eu/environment/nature/ecosystems/docs/green_infrastructure_broc.pdf. [18]

ECLAC (2012), *Population, Territory and Sustainable Development*, Economic Commission for Latin America and the Caribbean. [3]

Government of the Federal District (2017), *Water crisis leads government to declare emergency situation*, https://agenciabrasilia.df.gov.br/2017/01/25/crise-hidrica-leva-governo-a-decretar-situacao-de-emergencia/ (accessed on 15 December 2021). [27]

IBGE (2015), *National Sample Survey of Households*, tituto Brasileiro de Geografia e Estatística, https://biblioteca.ibge.gov.br/visualizacao/livros/liv98887.pdf. [2]

KPMG/ABICON (2020), *Quanto Custa Universalizar o Saneamento no Brasil*, https://conteudo.abconsindcon.com.br/kpmg. [12]

McDonald, R. and D. Shemie (2014), *Urban Water Blueprint: Mapping Conservation Solutions to the Global Water Challenge*, The Nature Conservancy, https://www.nature.org/content/dam/tnc/nature/en/documents/Urban_Water_Blueprint.pdf. [21]

MDR (2020), *National Sanitation Information System - SINIS*, http://www.snis.gov.br/painel-informacoes-saneamento-brasil/web/painel-esgotamento-sanitario. [7]

Ministry of Regional Development (2021), *Departamento Nacional de Obras Contra as Secas*, https://www.gov.br/dnocs/pt-br. [17]

Ministry of Regional Development (2021), *Perguntas Frequentes (Frequent Questions)*, https://www.codevasf.gov.br/acesso-a-informacao/perguntas-frequentes. [16]

MRD (2019), *PLANSAB, 2019. National Sanitation Plan*, https://antigo.mdr.gov.br/images/stories/ArquivosSDRU/ArquivosPDF/Versao_Conselhos_Resolu%C3%A7%C3%A3o_Alta_-_Capa_Atualizada.pdf. [11]

OECD (2021), *Water Governance in Peru*, OECD Studies on Water, OECD Publishing, Paris, https://dx.doi.org/10.1787/568847b5-en. [26]

OECD (2017), *Water Charges in Brazil: The Ways Forward*, OECD Studies on Water, OECD Publishing, Paris, https://dx.doi.org/10.1787/9789264285712-en. [25]

OECD (2015), *OECD Principles on Water Governance*, OECD, Paris, http://www.oecd.org/cfe/regional-policy/OECD-Principles-on-Water-Governance.pdf. [14]

OECD (2015), *Water and Cities: Ensuring Sustainable Futures*, OECD Studies on Water, OECD Publishing, paris, http://dx.doi.org/10.1787/9789264230149-en. [22]

OECD (2015), *Water Resources Allocation: Sharing Risks and Opportunities*, OECD Studies on Water, OECD Publishing, Paris, https://doi.org/10.1787/9789264229631-en. [13]

OECD (2015), *Water Resources Governance in Brazil*, OECD Studies on Water, OECD Publishing, Paris, https://dx.doi.org/10.1787/9789264238121-en. [15]

OECD (2013), "Barriers to, and Incentives for, the Adoption of Green Water Infrastructure", OECD, Paris. [20]

OECD/ANA (2019-21), "Water Governance Workshops". [23]

Siwi/Unicef/World Bank (2020), "The fundamental role of sanitation and hygiene promotion in the response to to Covid-19 in Brazil", https://documents1.worldbank.org/curated/en/998851596650728051/pdf/O-Papel-Fundamental-do-Saneamento-e-da-Promocao-da-Higiene-na-Resposta-a-Covid-19-no-Brasil.pdf. [5]

Trata Brasil (2020), "Future demand for treated water in Brazilian cities - 2017 to 2040". [4]

UNEP (2014), *Green Infrastructure Guide for Water Management: Ecosystem-based Management Approaches for Water-related Infrastructure Projects*, United Nations Environment Programme. [19]

WHO/UNICEF (2021), *Joint Monitoring Programme for Water Supply and Sanitation*, https://washdata.org/ (accessed on 17 December 2021). [6]

Annex 1.A. Action plan

The tables summarise the main actions presented in Chapter 1.

Annex Table 1.A.1. Governing water infrastructure for greater resilience

Strengthen governance and institutional arrangements	Strengthen the relationship between all relevant institutions. The Ministry of Regional Development, to which ANA belongs, should have a central role in relation to water infrastructure, with the engagement of entities simultaneously relevant to water resources management and to the social and economic development of the country, such as the CODEVASF (Company for the Development of São Francisco and Parnaíba Valleys) and DNOCS (National Department of Infrastructure against Droughts), both linked to the Ministry of Regional Development.
	Set a legislative basis for green infrastructure and cross-sector strategic engagement. The extent of the policy ambition for green infrastructure as a climate change adaptation measure needs to be agreed between relevant ministries. Planning, funding and delivering green infrastructure must be more formal, with legislative and budgetary support, and clear accountability for delivery depending on the nature of the scheme. An optimised portfolio of grey and green infrastructure appears critical to build and sustain water security and resilience.
Aim for resilience	Include worst-case scenarios for the potential impact of climate change and levels of future water demand. ANA made progress in understanding and managing risks to water supplies, and this approach now needs to include resilience thinking so that the duration and magnitude of failures is minimised. This assessment should then inform water planning, along the lines of 'hoping for the best but planning for the worst'. This will help identify capacity gaps and technical skills to be addressed and prioritise spending.
	Assess system vulnerabilities to shocks such as more extreme droughts than those planned for, or from cyber-attacks and telemetry failures. Also, consider measures implemented to mitigate impacts.
	Ensure greater reliability and resilience of existing supply systems, and introducing a wider range of source types less vulnerable to drought.
	Develop drought management plans for new and existing assets. It is important to develop drought management plans that set out accountabilities and actions agreed in advance with stakeholders across all sectors. Plans would help manage demand, with defined triggers for each step as drought intensifies. Where emergency resources can be utilised, it is important to agree on the conditions for their use and any mitigation measures to offset environmental and social impacts. Drought management plans contribute to moving from crisis management to risk management, as they require risk assessments, monitoring, and clear decision-making based on a series of indicators.
Ensure policy coherence	Initiate cross-departmental dialogues between ministries, such as establishing a permanent commission for policy integration to enhance cross-sectoral coherence and identify multiple benefits from every policy decision which could impact water directly or indirectly. A permanent commission for integrated planning would ensure that the impact of plans on each other is considered explicitly, and synergies, gaps and adverse impacts identified.
	Extend the concept of integrated work into routine practice. There is currently no institutional model to deliver an integrated approach to planning horizontally across different ministries and vertically between layers of government in order to overcome the fragmented approach and lack of clear accountability. Each level of government needs to have clear accountability for communicating and delivering on its role.
	Take into account the implications of wider policy decisions for water supply and sanitation, and taking proactive measures at an early stage in the planning process so that water becomes an enabler rather than a hurdle. Policy and legislation for municipal developments should consider water impacts, with developers and development authorities accountable for funding the additional demand they put on water infrastructure and ensuring that construction meets standards for water efficiency and minimising surface water runoff.
	Make a policy decision on levels of service for public water supply and other key sectors (i.e., an acceptable frequency of failure, such as during a once-a-century drought), and to confirm sectoral priorities during water emergencies, besides those already set by Law No. 9.433/1997, changed by Law No.14.026.
Build capacities	Address technical capacity through structured training programmes at an appropriate scale to ensure the operation and maintenance of sophisticated water supply systems and treatment processes. Technical capacities at municipal and state levels could be developed or strengthened to assess the effectiveness and efficiency of wastewater treatment and drinking water delivery against international standards for drinking water quality and pollution limits, and benchmark costs with other countries.
	Pilot different approaches to skills development to ensure consistent professional standards across the country.
	Develop training courses for river basin committee members to help them understand the complexities of water management and the trade-offs involved in decisions. For example, where there are large numbers of stakeholders in a particular sector, such as irrigators, the training could help make it clear that a user association would be able to speak

	for them and have more influence on decision-making.
	Set up mechanisms to share best practices within and between states, together with structured programmes for the continued professional development of staff. This could be done through virtual networks and discussion fora for specialists in particular disciplines, or periodic conferences or workshops to present case studies and encourage peer-to-peer learning.
	Consider how professional institutions could assess and recognise competence, and support continued professional development.
	Consider the benefits from the amalgamation of delivery bodies to provide efficiencies through economies of scale and adoption of best practices. Municipalities, particularly smaller ones, are vulnerable when technical skills are offered by just a few individuals, so sharing resources and amalgamating training can increase resilience.
Improve data collection and analysis	Produce and collect good data for managing water and assessing the potential of different options beyond grey infrastructure. Water security planning requires a broad range of data across different disciplines, such as hydrology, ecology, demographics and social science. It is essential to review the data needs for water supply security planning and establish the mechanisms to collect and store it so that it is accessible for use within a water planning process that takes account of climate change and adopts a twin track approach: implementing demand management measures in tandem with cultivating resource options.
	Integrate data collection and planning processes with a clear overall purpose. Long-tern planning (10-yearly with a 30-year horizon) already exists within the power sector and could be a model for water, which would also need to ensure that it is integrated with national development strategies. Having a single entity to oversee it could be beneficial.
	Use scenarios can help understand risk and uncertainty, and what contingencies might be needed if reality deviates significantly from the plan. The PNSH should be tested for risk, resilience and uncertainties using scenarios for different levels of demand and for water availability under climate change on timescales that are compatible with the expected life of water infrastructure.
	Perform cost-benefit analysis of the performance of infrastructure should be carried out to define if remedial works are needed, or whether low-cost improvements such as better control systems would allow it to perform better. The cost-benefit assessment for a new scheme should therefore consider a 'Do Nothing' option to see whether the capital and associated operational costs for O&M are more cost-effective and sustainable when the money is spent on improving and maintaining existing infrastructure, or on managing demand so as to negate the need for additional infrastructure.
Fund the multi-purpose operation and maintenance of water infrastructure	Clarify responsibility for O&M, transferring it to state governments, as is not currently the case, and increasing stakeholder involvement.
	Apply preventative maintenance so that assets function more reliably and are cheaper in the long run than assets that have not been properly maintained and fail repeatedly or catastrophically. Implementing a programme of routine preventative maintenance for water supply and wastewater assets would help ensure that they can reliably deliver target levels of service to customers.
	Condition the availability of federal funding for state and municipal priorities on regulatory compliance and the effective operation and maintenance of water infrastructure.
	Explore other mechanisms for funding, including use of the Land Tax as a mechanism for funding some water infrastructure, such as for flood risk management, and the potential for developers to help fund the consequent water impacts. There is a risk that funding water infrastructure is viewed as the responsibility of one government department or ministry. However, the constructed assets may provide a much wider benefit. As such, a more structured and explicit approach to funding the development and maintenance of water infrastructure from different budget streams may be justified.
	Apply different tariff structures on a sectoral or geographic (scarcity) basis. In this case, some issues to be taken into account are: the degree of water scarcity; the level of environmental sensitivity and degree of ecosystem stress; the proportion of used water that returned to a location where it could be reused; and effluent quality. It is also key to identify how to safeguard low-income and vulnerable households and other users, such as through cross-subsidies, social tariffs, income support or special rebates or discounts.
	Agree on restriction rules and compensation fund: there is general agreement that Brazil needs to have plans in place before a crisis so that actions, accountabilities and desired outcomes are clear at each pre-determined stage of a drought, mitigation measures are established, and the rules for restricting use have been agreed. The process for doing so should be inclusive and have a formalised governance system.
	Set up incentives and penalties to ensure that infrastructure is properly maintained and operated. Droughts and supply failures have an economic and social cost for both urban citizens and agriculture, but this is difficult to quantify. There is a perception by some that previous droughts have affected some sectors unevenly (agriculture in particular) but there is little culture of preventative planning. Incentives and penalties may be needed.
	Revise subsidies is important to understand whether agricultural subsidies are leading to poor water management or unsustainable farming practice, which could have an adverse impact on water resources, such as from the use of fertilisers and biocides causing pollution. Extending the application of the Water Producer Programme across more river basins could be also considered.
	Improve transparency about the need for these decisions at the highest levels of government. The availability of funding will always be a constraint on the level of service ambition, but greater transparency on what is being provided could make it easier to move towards levels of charging that support O&M as well as new capital investment.

Develop demand management	Understand the actions needed to manage demand in different sectors, such as industry and agriculture, and in the case of domestic water use.
	Establish mechanisms to share resources equitably and efficiently. A good start would be to assess the potential benefits of different demand management techniques and develop a demand management strategy and communication programme to reach all sectors, with a delivery plan to implement the actions with the greatest potential without delay.
	Create a demand management culture where water is regarded as a scarce and valuable resource. Techniques such as the use of tariffs or the introduction of more water-efficient fixtures, fittings and appliances, coupled with education and awareness-raising could all help create this culture. The application of tariffs could depend on the use, water scarcity or environmental impact, and there should be safeguards for those who would struggle to pay for an essential service.
	Define targets for water efficiency to drive action. For this to be effective, however, there needs to be a coherent demand management and communications strategy in place, and agreed mechanisms for equitable allocation and charging.
	Assess the potential benefits of different demand management techniques and developing a demand management strategy and communication programme to reach all sectors, with a delivery plan to implement the actions with greatest potential without delay. This should include a programme of leakage reduction with performance targets, benchmarked against international good practice together with programmes of awareness-raising to improve the efficiency of industrial and agricultural processes. Household demand management could also include education and awareness raising, the distribution of water efficient fixtures and fittings such as low-flow shower heads and cistern displacement devices, water efficiency labelling of appliances, and nudge messaging on bills. Regulatory penalties and incentives could be applied in the most water-scarce areas.
Engage stakeholders	Encourage greater participation by stakeholders in operational and investment decisions, which might imply developing the capability of existing river basin committees. Where there are large numbers of stakeholders in one sector, such as irrigators, they are likely to have more influence on decision-making if they belong to a user association that is able to speak for them. For dialogue to be effective there would also need to be clear sectoral policies to determine priorities and agree the level of funding and standard of service for each sector.
	Facilitate stakeholder consultation and engagement on the regulation and management of each scheme, with clearly identified roles and accountabilities. This will help ensure that changes in demand and water availability are managed sustainably and transparently.

Note

[1] Green infrastructure (GI) is a nature-based solution encompassing all actions that rely on ecosystems and the services they provide to respond to societal challenges such as climate change, food security and disaster risk.

2 Strengthening multi-level governance and the use of economic instruments in the Piancó-Piranhas Açu River Basin

This chapter provides a deep dive into the specific case of the Piancó-Piranhas Açu River Basin as a testbed to address broader water governance and financing challenges in Brazil. Due to its economic and hydrological characteristics, the Piancó-Piranhas Açu River Basin is fragile in terms of securing present and future water supply. Despite a robust institutional and legal structure, implementation gaps remain in ensuring that governance arrangements fulfil water management functions. This chapter suggests options to improve multi-level governance at the basin level and economic instruments in view of the implementation of the São Francisco Integration Project (PISF), which will transfer water to the basin and bring substantial changes to the water management landscape.

Hydrological features of the Piancó-Piranhas Açu basin

The Piancó-Piranhas Açu (PPA) Interstate River Basin covers 46 683 km² of semi-arid territory in the Northeast region of Brazil (Figure 2.1). The PPA river basin hosts 1.4 million people on 43 000 km², part of the states of Paraíba (60% of the basin) and Rio Grande do Norte (40%) (IBGE, 2011[1]).

Figure 2.1. The Piancó-Piranhas Açu River Basin

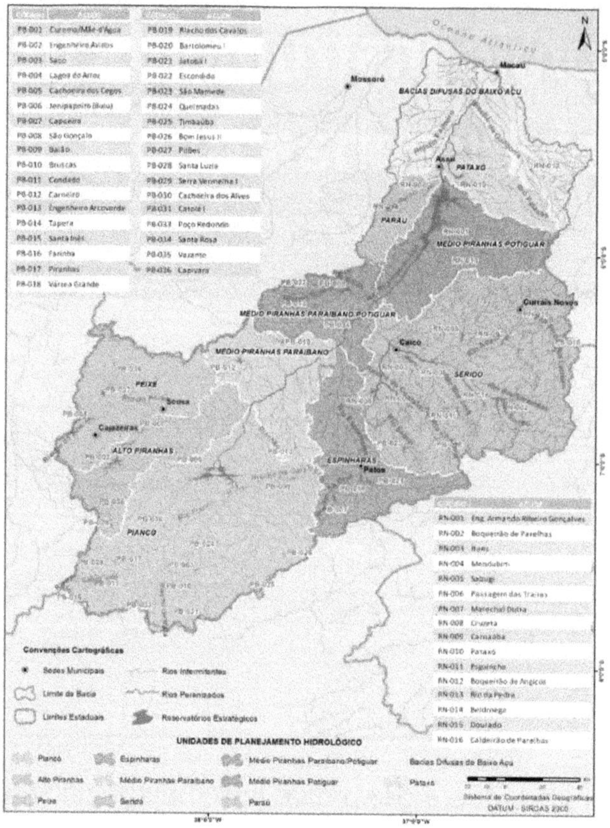

Source: ANA (2016[2]), "Plano de recursos hídricos da bacia hidrográfica do rio Piancó-Piranhas-Açu", http://piranhasacu.ana.gov.br/produtos/PRH_PiancoPiranhasAcu_ResumoExecutivo_30062016.pdf.

Due to its socio-economic and hydrological characteristics, the basin is very fragile in terms of securing water supply now and in the future. The basin's hydro-climatology is characterised by a rainy season that goes from January to June (yearly rainfall ranges from 440 to 1 050 mm) and the absence of rain during the rest of the year, combined with multi-year drought periods that occur periodically. From 2012 to 2020, the basin experienced one of its worst periods of severe multi-year drought (de Sousa Freitas, 2021[3]). Most rivers are intermittent, thus almost all water supply is provided by several reservoirs that total a storage capacity of 5 352 hm³. Some of these reservoirs operate to maintain river flow and serve as a source of water for irrigators, public water supply and others.

There are three major reservoirs in the PPA river basin, namely the Curema-Mãe d'Agua (CMA, 1 160 hm³), the Armando Ribeiro Gonçalves (ARG, 2 400 hm³) and the Engenheiro Ávidos (EA, 400 hm³), corresponding to 70% of the storage capacity of surface water in the basin (5 659 hm³) (Figure 2.2). The CMA provides water to the Várzea de Souza irrigation district (2 610 hectares in irrigated area plus water supply to two cities totalling 65 000 inhabitants) and regulates flow in a 165 km downstream river reach that serves as the water source to 465 000 inhabitants and more than 4 000 hectares that can be irrigated on 1 250 farms. The ARG is the direct water source for long pipeline systems that provide water to many cities totalling 400 000 inhabitants within and out of the basin. In addition, it regulates flow in the 70 km downstream reach, which provides water to the Baixo Açu irrigation district (2 400 hectares of irrigated area) and 3 766 hectares of irrigated farms taking water from the river, and several aquaculture farms (mainly producing shrimp) totalling 630 hectares in fish tank area. In 2012, there were 54.4 thousand hectares of irrigated land, corresponding to 1.3% of the river basin drainage area. The major temporary agriculture areas produce soybean and maize, while the permanent agriculture areas produce banana and coconuts (ANA, 2016[2]).

Figure 2.2. Reservoir systems in the Piancó-Piranhas Açu River Basin

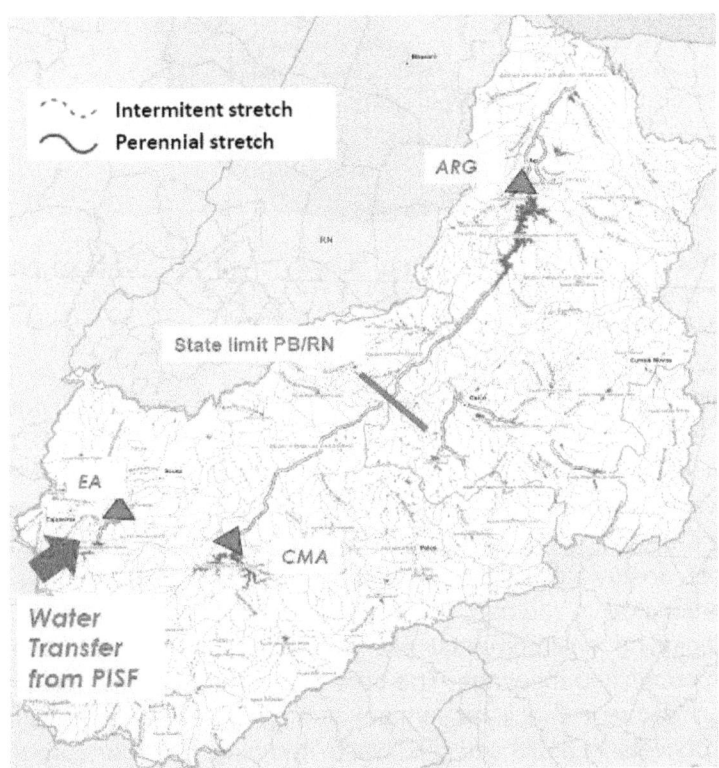

Source: based on ANA (2016[2]), *Plano de recursos hídricos da bacia hidrográfica do rio Piancó-Piranhas-Açu - Resumo executivo* / Water resources plan of the Piancó- Piranhas-Açu basin – Executive Summary, http://piranhasacu.ana.gov.br/produtos/PRH_PiancoPiranhasAcu_ResumoExecutivo_30062016.pdf.

Despite the reservoirs, 60% (31 out of 52) of the hydrological planning units[1] in the PPA river basin have a negative water supply/demand balance (ANA, 2016[2]). The water resource of the basin aquifers is limited (annual recharge of 458 hm^3, equivalent to 8% of the water stored in reservoirs) and little used (93 hm^3 or 20% of the annual recharge). Irrigation accounts for two thirds of water demand, fish farming 22%, public water supply 7%, industry and livestock share the remaining 4% (ANA, 2016[2]). There is a lack of investment in water security (e.g. dams, reservoirs, wastewater collection and treatment), due to the limited capacity to invest in the basin. Therefore, targeted measures are needed to enhance the basin's resilience, cope with supply and pollution issues, and competition across water users.

Irrigated agriculture is one of the main economic activities and has been key to regional development since the 1970s. The irrigated area is about 81 000 hectares (IBGE, 2006[4]). Irrigators are the main water users (65.7%), followed by aquaculture (23.6%), human consumption (7.6%), industry (1.6%) and livestock (1.5%) (Figure 2.3).

Figure 2.3. Water use in the Piancó-Piranhas Açu River Basin, per sector

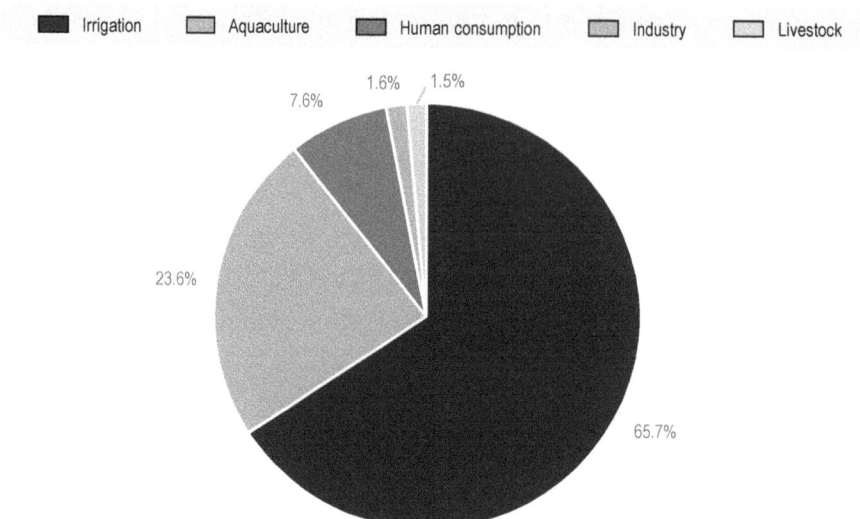

Source: ANA (2014[5]), Cadernos de Capacitação em Recursos Hídricos - Volume 07: Cobrança pelo uso de recursos hídricos, https://capacitacao.ana.gov.br/conhecerh/handle/ana/10 and CBH PPA (n.d.[6]), Relatorio, http://cbhpiancopiranhasacu.org.br/docs/relatorio/tdrplanopiranhasacu_final-1.pdf .

Water pollution is a significant challenge for the Piancó-Piranhas Açu river basin due to insufficient sewage treatment and fertiliser runoff (ANA, 2014[5]; ANA, 2016[7]; IBGE, 2006[4]; IBGE, 2011[1]). About 96% of the urban population has access to drinking water in the State of Paraíba and 92% in the State of Rio Grande do Norte. However, sewage collection rates are much lower in the State of Paraíba (2.46%) and the State of Rio Grande do Norte (13.95%) (ANA, 2014[5]) (CBH PPA, n.d.[6]). The main cause of polluted water in the area is lack of proper wastewater treatment, which comes under the responsibility of municipalities. The municipalities face constraints (human, technical and financial) and despite their important role in managing sanitation, including environmental licensing and solid waste management, they seldom participate in river basin committee meetings. The poor engagement of municipalities in water resources management, a common feature in Brazil, hinders any strategic vision for the basin. In addition, the basin culture enables the use of rivers for liquid and solid waste dumping. There are programmes at federal level to support municipalities in the sanitation sector, which is their responsibility.

Increasing water security through the São Francisco Integration Project

An ambitious infrastructure project

The São Francisco River transfer, known as the São Francisco Integration Project (PISF), will reduce uncertainty over water availability in the PPA. In 2007, Brazil launched the PISF and began building its infrastructure to boost economic development in the northeast of the country, including the PPA basin. The PISF is the most expensive Brazilian hydraulic infrastructure to date, expected to reach BRL 12 billion (USD 5.8 billion) (da Silva Santos, 2021[8]). Originally scheduled for completion by 2011, the project experienced several delays and cost overruns. Currently in the final phase of execution, the project aims to divert 1.4% of the largest river located exclusively in Brazil to the semi-arid zones of north-eastern Brazil, which are home to 29% of the Brazilian population but only have 3.3% of the country's water resources. It also aims to help the Northeast hydraulic network operate in a more synergistic way (hence the reference in the project name to integration rather than diversion).

The São Francisco River is set to provide water to some of the driest regions of its semi-arid Northeast region. Six river basins will benefit from the project: Jaguaribe (Ceará), Piranhas-Açu and Apodi (Rio Grande do Norte), and Paraíba, Moxotó and Brígida (Pernambuco). According to the Brazilian Ministry of Regional Development, the PISF will assure the supply needs of municipalities in the semi-arid Agreste Pernambucano and Fortaleza Metropolitan region, and would be the solution to the problems brought about by the scarcity of water and severe droughts.

The PISF consists of two independent systems of canals, pipelines and aqueducts (the north axis and the east axis) which extend for approximately 720 km (Figure 2.4). The north axis transfers the waters of the São Francisco River to the basins of the Jaguaribe (Ceara), Piranhas-Açu (Rio Grande do Norte) and Apodi-Mossoro (Rio Grande do Norte) rivers. The east axis connects to the basin of the Paraíba River (Paraíba) and to some basins of Pernambuco (via the Ramal do Agreste, the largest water infrastructure project in Pernambuco). The east axis was the first to come into service, in 2017, and currently supplies five reservoirs in the Paraíba River basin (de Lucena Barbosa et al., 2021[9]).

The project also creates momentum for taking action on pressing issues such as water pollution and freshwater contamination, to which water charges can contribute. The project is implemented by the Ministry of Regional Development with a USD 3 billion budget. Revenues from water charges could contribute to its operability and maintenance. However, with the progress of its implementation, addressing water governance issues in the PPARB becomes even more urgent as PISF will bring substantial changes in the water management landscape requiring the institutional development of government agencies, river basin organisms and operational institutions responsible for hydrologic monitoring, water use control and reservoir operations.

Figure 2.4. Northern and eastern routes of the São Francisco water transfer project

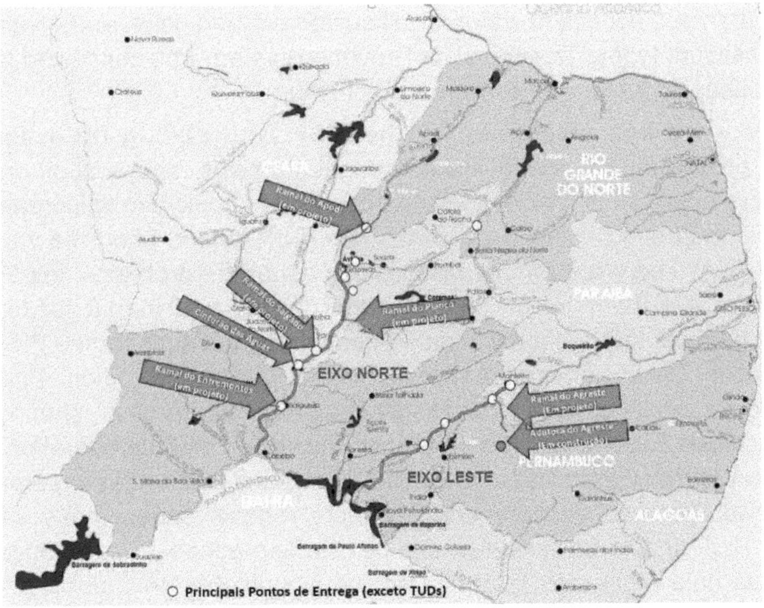

Source: Ministério da Integração Nacional, (2004[10]), Relatório de Impacto Ambiental da Transposição. Brasília.

Towards successful implementation of the São Francisco Integration Project

The first phase of the PISF is now in place and starting to highlight issues relating to the operation and maintenance (O&M) of major water infrastructure. The federal government was responsible for financing and delivering the construction phase, establishing the management system and defining the operator at federal level. The states are responsible for O&M and water use. The idea was that the states would charge beneficiaries and provide funds for the operator. Under a contractual arrangement, state water agencies

(AESA and IGARN, which are state operators) in both Paraíba and Rio Grande do Norte should pay the PISF federal operator (CODEVASF, Development Company of the São Francisco and Parnaíba Valleys) to receive bulk water from PISF. However, there is no legal provision allowing AESA and IGARN to recover these costs from end users. For federal reservoirs, the federal government (DNOCS, National Department of Works Against Droughts of the Ministry of Regional Development) fully supports O&M costs. Moreover, energy costs are a major operational expense. They vary over the year, making tariff setting very challenging. There is a need to look for operational efficiencies and cheaper sources of energy.

The successful implementation of PISF requires an institutional arrangement that allows for the coordination of federal and state roles, the effective management of the transferred resource, and an efficient and secure financing system. Full commercial operation has not yet commenced, so the resolution of outstanding issues is urgently needed.

Following several best practices (Box 2.1), the following should be considered:

- **Formalising institutional arrangements for decision making** for the regulation and management of the PISF scheme, so that roles and accountabilities are clear and changes in demand and water availability are managed sustainably. The design and operation of schemes requires coordination across all levels of government, and the involvement of beneficiaries and other stakeholders. The example of the Société du Canal de Provence (SCP) in France provides an inspirational example of a possible governance arrangement for the PISF. The SCP is a semi-public company created in 1957 as a Regional Development Company, benefiting from a stable shareholding structure, with over 80% of shares held by local authorities. In 1963, the SCP signed a 75-year concession to build and operate the Provence Canal. Within the framework of the concession awarded by the *Région Sud Provence-Alpes-Côte d'Azur*, the SCP's primary task was to manage and ensure a secure water supply for Provence. To do so, it designed a state-of-the-art network to guarantees access to water for all customers and uses, and continues to develop and maintain this network today. The Canal de Provence system was conceived to allow adaptation to demand, thus keeping water withdrawals to a minimum.

- **Clarifying the aims and objectives for the PISF, and setting up a communications and engagement programme** for beneficiaries so that the basis for operation and funding is clear to all. The project's objective is regional development, so it should aim to increase welfare by making water available to support economic growth. The PISF helped bring the various states together and closer to ANA. There are regular discussions about the problems, but these have so far not been able to resolve them, which suggests that the current format for dialogue needs to be reconsidered, perhaps through a think tank. In particular, the aims for the PISF need to be agreed in terms of priority beneficiaries and strategic objectives for the region. Ultimately, the dialogue should lead to contribute to the financial sustainability of the project, sharing costs and benefits across beneficiaries. Experience from overseas has shown that the operation of transfer schemes needs to be considered dynamically, so that it can respond to changes in demand, climate change, extremes of weather and environmental impacts. These issues make it imperative that the objectives for PISF should be reviewed, and flexible operational rules established that do not lock the system into rigid processes that may not be sustainable. In Colombia, behavioural change campaigns in the Valle de Cauca contributed to doubling the number of downstream water users implementing conservation measures. Fourteen staff of the local environmental authority trained community leaders in natural resource management, social marketing and campaign planning, while also building their capacity to create trust among different types of stakeholders. As a result, about 1 700 ha of forest are now protected voluntarily by landowners in the region. Valle de Cauca exceeded its annual conservation goal, deforestation rates sank well below the national average and the watersheds see positive trends in the forest and water quality indices.

- **Testing the PISF for risk, resilience and uncertainties using scenarios for different levels of demand** and water availability under climate change over timescales compatible with the expected life of water infrastructure (i.e., at least 50 years). Consider how a more integrated portfolio of options, such as greater use of demand management, leakage reduction, effluent reuse, desalination or groundwater, could help manage risk and uncertainty. Like the Canal de Provence and associated infrastructure, the focus is on supply, with investments planned decades (if not centuries) ago, rather than demand (water efficiency, water use reduction). However, given the technical solutions available now and the increasing awareness, including in the agricultural sector, a shift from supply to demand management should be considered.

- **Initiating a programme of engagement and awareness-raising** so that good practice for rules of access and charges are in place when full operation starts. The PISF will not offer unlimited free water. Discussions about what a perfect tariff structure should look like risk preventing the implementation of some form of charging. There is a perception that the communities who stand to benefit believe that the water is available to them at zero cost because they have had no communication about the aims and operation of the scheme.

- **Establishing rules for access to the resource, supported by a system of permits and compliance monitoring** to encourage users to operate efficiently and minimise wastage. These issues are interlinked, and it is essential that there is a dialogue with all stakeholders in order to reach a resolution on the arrangements for governance and funding. If these matters are not resolved the result will be lack of funds for O&M, deterioration in asset condition, and a failure to deliver the intended welfare and economic benefits of this major scheme.

- **Using water charges to demonstrate that the water has value and there is a cost to making it available** and maintaining the assets that provide it. There are fixed costs with all major schemes, and variable ones relating to fluctuations in demand, which ultimately should be funded by those who benefit from an increased security of supply, or from a new supply. The priority beneficiaries are the water customers in the municipalities, who should pay a realistic charge for their water service, subject to safeguards for those for whom affordability is an issue. The PISF will need to operate at capacity to reach all areas with irrigation potential, and there is a belief that users will appear when the water is available. Improved governance arrangements and transparency in tariffs could achieve the original objective of PISF (see next section).

- **Developing a programme for the technical monitoring of the performance of the PISF** and other major schemes to review control rules as necessary and inform schedules and budgets for routine and preventative maintenance, so that losses are minimised and all parts of the transfer system operate as designed. Monitor the system on an ongoing basis for impacts, including environmental, hydrological, socio-economic and regional, so that operating rules can be modified to reduce adverse and unforeseen impacts. With all major schemes, it is essential that there is ongoing monitoring of performance so that control rules can be reviewed and revised as necessary to ensure that they are operating as intended, and so that routine and preventative maintenance can be scheduled efficiently. The scheme was constructed in the hope that increasing the security of water supplies would materialise demand to take advantage of the additional resource. An average flow of up to 26.4 m^3/second is guaranteed for human and animal supplies. If not all of this is used, it can be allocated for other purposes. Depending on the level in the Sobradinho dam, up to 127 m^3/s can be available. The distribution of flows between different user sectors and states, and the charges to be levied, are specified in the Annual Management Plan, which is approved by ANA. Without tight controls and regulation of formal allocation, and enforcement to minimise unlawful use, there is a risk that uncontrolled expansion of use will impact on contracted and priority use. However, increased use brings with it the potential to earn more revenue to cover costs, although this will be offset by increased operational (primarily energy) costs. The example of the Tagus-Segura transfer in Spain demonstrates that environmental impacts might only become apparent over long timescales, so there needs to be a comprehensive, long-term monitoring commitment to understand the effect on flows, water quality and ecosystems.

Box 2.1. International experience of large water transfer schemes

Water transfers in Spain

The Tagus-Segura transfer is a scheme linking the Bolarque Reservoir on the Tagus River in central Spain with the Talave Reservoir on the Segura River in the dry southeast of the country. It is 292 km long and capable of transferring up to 33 m³/s. Its design was based upon the river flow series from 1958-79, which suggested that up to 1,000 hm³/annum was feasible. However, since 1979 flows in the donor basin have declined by 47% and the volume thought to be available for transfer was reduced to 600 hm³/a. In practice, transfers have averaged only 351 hm³/a. One third of the water is used for public supply and the remainder for irrigation. Evaporation and other losses account for about 20 hm³/a.

Despite its economic benefits in the Segura basin, the transfer resulted in significant adverse impacts in both donor and recipient basins. In the Tagus, there were major changes in the river dynamics, increased erosion and reduction of water quality. This deterioration sparked social and political concern. The Segura ecosystems were impacted by the introduction of non-native species of fish, which are dominating local fish populations. In addition, the increase in irrigation caused groundwater levels to rise and become increasingly polluted by nutrients. These impacts led to discussions about how best to manage large transfers, and the need for continuous adaptation.

This experience provides some useful lessons transferable to the PISF:

- Feasibility should be tested under different rainfall and socio-economic scenarios.
- Transfers can create a range of impacts in the affected basins, which should be identified as part of the environmental assessment for the scheme. If they materialise after construction and during operation, they must be addressed and minimised.
- Transfers are very sensitive to climatic change and shifts in social dynamics.
- Effective inter-administrative cooperation is key for sustainable operation of the transfer.

Large scale water infrastructure in the UK

In the UK, there are numerous water transfers in place, some dating from the late 19th Century and supplying cities in the north and west of the country. These assets were largely funded by the municipalities that commissioned the works, but operating and maintenance costs are now the responsibility of private water companies, which have taken over that responsibility from the public sector. Their costs are recovered fully from charges to their customers. In some cases, the water and environmental regulator, which has a similar role ANA, is responsible for the operation and maintenance where assets benefit multiple sectors. In these cases, costs are covered fully by charges levied on abstractors, who pay a premium for the benefit of abstracting water from a regulated river system.

No major water supply infrastructure was commissioned in the past 40 years; any proposals to do so were subject to strong opposition from local communities and green NGO's. However, a severe drought in 2010-12, which threatened water security in London, led to recognition that investment was needed. Private water companies collaborated to develop a national water security plan for England. Regulators and government gave guidance that this must adopt a twin-track approach and combine demand management measures with resource development, and must take account of the potential impacts of climate change on water availability, as well as environmental flow needs and demands from other sectors. The plan includes ambitious programmes for water efficiency and leakage control, and a broad mix of schemes such as greater connectivity within and between companies, dams, transfers, effluent reuse, groundwater, and desalination.

In each region, a water resources group was established to bring together all sectors and stakeholders to address the economic, social and environmental challenges. In time, these may support the operational management of resources, in a similar way to a long-established Consultative Committee for the River Dee in North Wales. This group was established in legislation to oversee the operation of a series of dams that provide regulate flow on the River Dee, which supports abstraction for public water supply by three companies, as well as navigation, irrigation and industry. The river is also important for its ecology and fishery, and the operational rules ensure that environmental flow needs are considered as a priority. There are rules for the operation of the system during droughts, with the impact shared across different sectors. In the event of a more severe drought than planned, the Committee works to obtain consensus on how restrictions on abstraction should operate.

The River Dee and similar systems provide ideas about how new schemes should be charged and operated. The immediate challenge is how the construction of any new schemes should be funded. With a privatised water sector, it is unlikely that government funding would be available, so it would fall to the companies to raise capital or for a third-party investor to own the scheme and get a return from the beneficiaries. For either of these options, there needs to be the certainty of a stable and adequate income base to pay interest on loans and provide a return on capital. There also needs to be a stable regulatory regime operating with the explicit support of government to give confidence to potential investors. Conversely, operators will need flexibility to optimise the use of assets. Where schemes also provide an environmental benefit, as is likely to be the case in England, the environmental regulator might need to fund the proportion of the costs involved.

A strategy for the Danube River

The Danube is the second longest river in Europe, with a basin that includes 19 countries in Central and Eastern Europe, meaning that it is the most international river basin in the world. It is important for navigation and hydropower, and is a major source of drinking water. It is also home to a critically endangered species of sturgeon, which migrate upstream to spawn. Hydropower installations and other barriers, together with over-exploitation of the fishery, mean that populations have declined significantly.

The ecological impact of hydropower led to tensions between conflicting interests, and resulted in shifts in policy thinking about the use of dams for water supply and hydropower. The International Commission for the Protection of the Danube River (ICPDR) was contracted in 2000 for the implementation of all the transboundary aspects of the Water Framework Directive, and in 2007 for the Floods Directive. Its aim is to safeguard the water resources of the Danube for future generations, to protect its water quality and ecology, and to minimise the impact of floods.

The ICPDR initiated a dialogue to develop Guiding Principles for Sustainable Hydropower Development in the Danube Basin. These set out a strategy, which includes identifying stretches of the Danube that should be kept free from hydropower development, and those where it would be likely to have minimal impact. Where existing structures are adapted or upgraded, measures should allow the passage of fish.

Although water availability in the Danube Basin has so far not been heavily affected by climate change, it will likely have significant impacts on water availability and demand (and navigability) in the future. This will likely add to pressures from irrigation and public water supply on dams and reservoirs. In addition, there is a need to reduce abstraction rates to protect ecological flows. Leakage rates in some countries within the basin are as high as 75%, so addressing these losses and improving the efficiency of use in others sectors such as irrigation could significantly benefit the river.

The next River Basin Management Plan for the Danube (2021-2027) will have to address and reconcile issues of water scarcity and environmental impacts of dams and reservoirs.

Source: OECD-ANA (2019-21[11]), "Water Governance Workshops".

Getting water governance right in the Piancó-Piranhas Açu River Basin

This section describes opportunities and recommendations based on normative OECD frameworks, studies and reviews on water governance and water management, and international best practices.

Adopting a governance arrangement that ensures water management at an appropriate scale and fosters coordination

The PPA river basin cuts across the States of Paraíba and Rio Grande do Norte. As of 2009, a single River Basin Committee (CBH) governs the PPA river basin, as agreed by the federal level and the two states. The states of Paraíba and Rio Grande do Norte have a Water Resources Councils (CERH), State Secretariats and water agencies – the Paraíba State Water Management Executive Agency (AESA) and the Rio Grande do Norte State Water Management Institute (IGARN). Mapping who does what is the first step in representing the allocation of roles and responsibilities at different levels of government and across functions for water resources management within the basin (Figure 2.5).

Roles and responsibilities across levels of government are allocated as follows:

- **Federal level**
    - The **National Water Resources Council** (CNRH) has deliberative powers, and is responsible for approving the National Water Plan and defining general directives for water management instruments, including water permitting and water charges.
    - The **National Water and Sanitation Agency** (ANA) is responsible for issuing water permits regarding federal waters. It is also in charge of hydrologic and reservoir monitoring, water use monitoring, control and enforcement, and water management projects at the federal level.
    - The **National Department of Works Against Droughts** (DNOCS) is a Federal Government department that manages 321 reservoirs in the Northeast of Brazil. Some of those reservoirs are in the Piancó-Piranhas-Açu River Basin and provide 70% of the basin's surface water.
    - The **Ministry for Regional Development** (MDR) is the major water infrastructure provider, responsible for policy formulation and implementation. It finances new water systems and dams.
    - The **São Francisco and Parnaiba Valleys Development Company** (CODEVASF) is the current federal operator of the PISF.
- **State level**
    - The **State Secretariats for the Environment, Water Resources and Science and Technology of Paraíba** and **Rio Grande do Norte** are responsible for water policy formulation and implementation, and for major water project financing at the state level. These secretariats also own reservoirs built by the state.
    - The **Executive Agency for Water Management of the State of Paraíba** (AESA) and the **Water Management Institute of the State of Rio Grande do Norte** (IGARN) are responsible for issuing permits for state waters. They are also in charge of hydrologic and reservoir monitoring, water use monitoring, control and enforcement, and water management projects at the State level. AESA also operates state-owned water systems.
    - The **Water Resources Councils of the States of Paraíba** (CERH/PB) and **Rio Grande do Norte** (CERH/RN) have deliberative powers, and are responsible for approving the State Water Plans and defining general directives for water management instruments, including water permitting and water charges at state level.

- **Basin level**
    - The **Piancó-Piranhas-Açu River Basin Committee** (PPA-RBC) was created in 2006 and started operating in 2009. The PPA-RBC is a water parliament gathering 40 representatives from water use sectors, governmental agencies and civil society. It is in charge of fostering discussion regarding water issues, approving the River Basin Management Plan, setting water use priorities, approving water charge methodologies and the implementation schedule.
    - Since the end of 2016, a **Technical Office** contracted by ANA was established in the PPARB as part of the implementation of the river basin plan. This Technical Office has been developing several operational functions to support water management and governmental agencies.

The Piancó-Piranhas-Açu River Basin Plan is a reference for the River Basin Committee and water resources management bodies of Federal and State rivers (see next section). Approved in 2016, the plan has a budget of BRL 150 million for the first five years and foresees three types of action – management, complementary studies, and projects – targeted at enhancing water security and quality due to the low level of sanitation infrastructure. Actions will be implemented by the River Basin Committee, ANA, AESA and IGARN. The PPA River Basin Plan was extended until 2021 and a basin plan revision is in preparation for the 5-year period from 2022. The main constraints that hinder the implementation of the PPA River Basin Plan are: (1) the ANA budget is the only source of funding for the CBH in the absence of a funding mechanism based on basin water users, and (2) PPA basin measures must be aligned with water policies at state and municipal levels.

In this context, roles and responsibilities need to be clearly defined and allocated, and strong coordination mechanisms put in place. Multi-level governance requires robust articulation between actors and objectives. It also requires strong participation mechanisms to ensure all entities are actively involved. The weak involvement of municipalities in water resource management, which derives primarily from the "double dominion" situation whereby the Brazilian Constitution divides ownership and competences over water resources between the Union (for rivers which cross state boundaries) and federal states, hinders a strategic vision for the PPA river basin.

In the PPA river basin, the choice between relying on existing state agencies and creating a new water management institution (i.e., a PPA Water Agency) is being discussed. To some extent, the problem is not about the institutional structure but rather about efficiently fulfilling water management functions (water quantity and drainage, water quality, flood defence, sewage management and wastewater treatment, and drinking water supply). Thus, it is important to ensure that the governance arrangement chosen bears the functions and powers to exercise its mission at the appropriate scale. As such:

- **Making use of existing structures could be more efficient.** In France, when creating the Water Agencies in 1964, these faced problems to hire competent and adequate personnel, hampering their capacity to fulfil their missions. These difficulties in building a new institution are already present in the PPA river basin as the lack of personnel in state water management and environmental agencies hinders operational capacity for inspections in the field. Creating a new institution could aggravate this situation. Moreover, the institutions in charge of water management in both Paraíba and Rio Grande do Norte States provide many levels of accountability, which can be considered positive.
- **Finding the smallest appropriate scale to fulfil water management functions could be a guiding principle.** Although each country has its own particularities, following the principle of subsidiarity could be a reference point.

Figure 2.5. Institutional mapping for water resources management in the Piancó-Piranhas Açu River Basin, Brazil

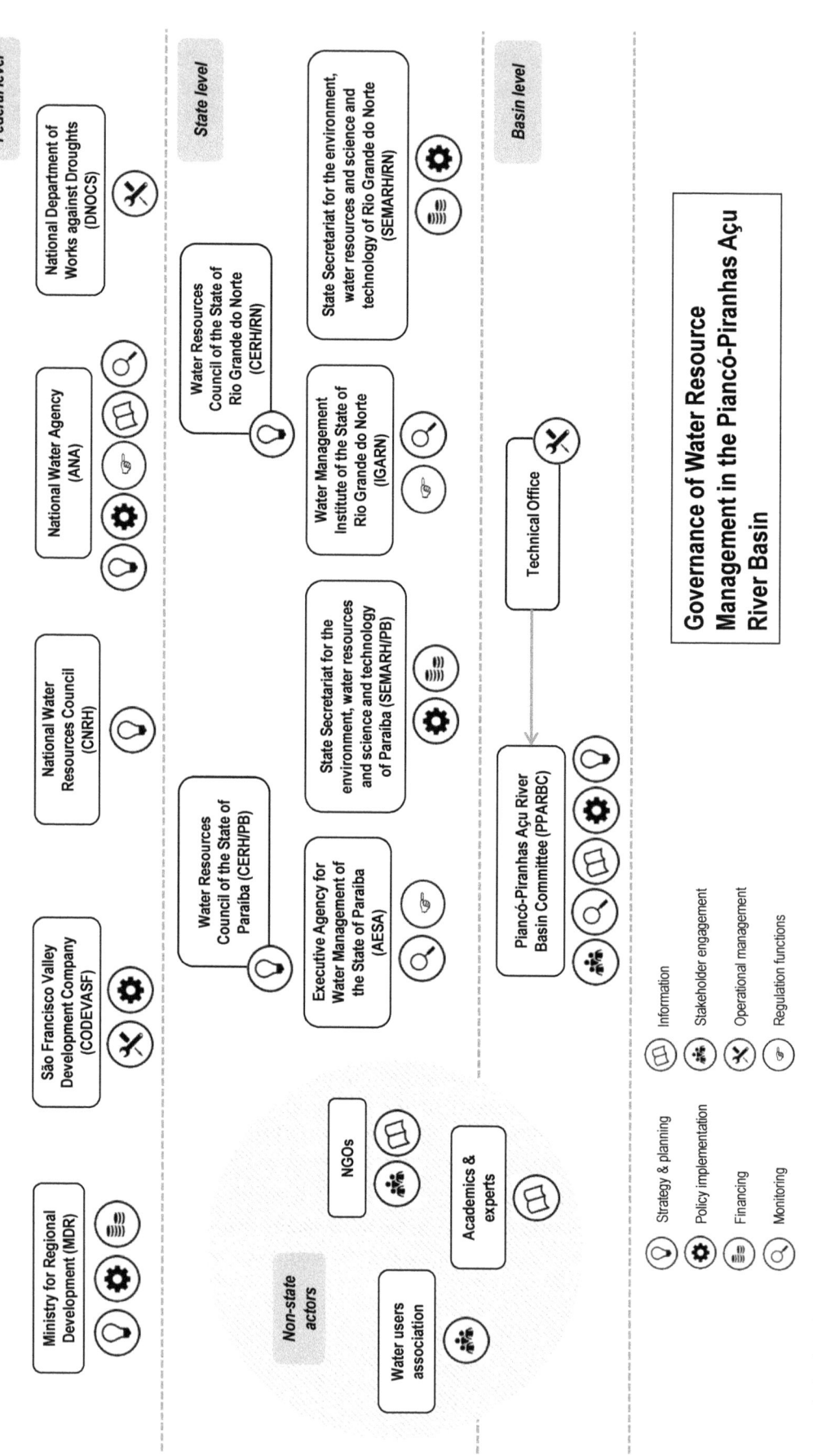

Source: Author's elaboration based on OECD (2011[12]), *Water Governance in OECD Countries: A Multi-level Approach*, https://doi.org/10.1787/9789264119284-en.

- **Evaluating whether catchment-based institutions are delivering on their mandate could identify gaps and strategically plan measures to overcome them.** An example is the self-assessment tool used in the United Republic of Tanzania to evaluate the performance of the nine basin water boards that implement IWRM at basin level. The basin water boards are decentralised administrative units, which together with catchment committees and water users' associations make up the institutional framework for water resources management. The Performance Assessment Framework is a self-assessment tool that supports basin water boards to regularly assess their performance against their institutional mandate. The tool was developed by the Ministry of Water and Irrigation with the support of the German Society for International Co-operation (Deutsche Gesellschaft für Internationale Zusammenarbeit, GIZ). The Ministry provides support to the boards when conducting the Performance Assessment Framework, which is also an excellent opportunity for the ministry to map the strengths and weaknesses of each (OECD, 2018[13]).

Strengthening stakeholder engagement

Strengthening stakeholder engagement at river basin level is key to fostering informed and outcome-oriented contributions to water policy design and implementation. Both formal and informal communications are important, and must occur regularly and consistently. In a tentative taxonomy, the OECD (2015[14]) describes some of the advantages and drawbacks that both formal and informal engagement mechanisms bring about (Box 2.2).

- **Formal** mechanisms such as water associations and river basin organisations are based on the principle of representative democracy, which confers legitimacy. However, they can be perceived as single-minded when they focus solely on pushing the agenda of a single group of stakeholders. River basin organisations can present challenges in terms of lobbying and consultation capture when discussions and decisions are monopolised by the interests of certain groups. They can also generate principle-agent tensions by which the person sitting at the table voices his/her own concern rather than representing his/her broader constituency. This should be a concern when selecting stakeholders to participate in advisory boards, working groups or assemblies.
- The **informal** nature of meetings and workshops can both foster deliberation and build a sense of community. They provide an open atmosphere that makes participants more willing to discuss issues and maximises dialogues that might not come to light through more structured mechanisms. For instance, meetings and workshops are flexible in timeframe and scale (from community meetings to international conferences) and can apply to a range of issues (e.g., from discussing a municipal sewer project to debating transboundary basin management agreements). They offer an opportunity for anyone to express concerns, access and share information, and gain better understanding. However, if tools to involve stakeholders do not have a minimum of structure and mediation, outcomes can be difficult to incorporate into decisions. Follow-up is also needed to turn views and concerns into contributions to decision-making beyond information sharing.

Box 2.2. OECD principles of stakeholder engagement for inclusive water governance

Critical aspects of governance should guide stakeholder engagement frameworks. Fair and equitable access to engagement opportunities is key to ensuring a balanced and representative process that takes account of diverse ideas and opinions. Being transparent and open about the ways to identify stakeholders, choose engagement mechanisms and define objectives can help raise interest among stakeholders and develop an understanding of and support for the final decisions. It is not sufficient to provide platforms for stakeholders to share their ideas; decision-makers must also demonstrate how these are taken into account. Procedural transparency and timely disclosure of information, including alternative solutions, are critical to ensuring the legitimacy of decision-making processes and their outcomes. Engagement can bring together groups with opposing views who fear that theirs will not be considered. Showing participants the intention of the process and how their input will be met is important to ensuring productive discussion and exchange of opinions. It is also important that decision-makers be able to trust the quality and value of input from non-technical experts (OECD, 2015[14]).

Table 2.1. OECD principles of stakeholder engagement for inclusive water governance

Inclusiveness and equity	Principle 1: Map all stakeholders who have a stake in the outcome or that are likely to be affected, as well as their responsibility, core motivations and interactions
Clarity of goals, transparency and accountability	Principle 2: Define the ultimate line of decision-making, the objectives of stakeholder engagement and the expected use of inputs
Capacity and information	Principle 3: Allocate proper financial and human resources and share needed information for results-oriented stakeholder engagement
Efficiency and effectiveness	Principle 4: Regularly assess the process and outcomes of stakeholder engagement to learn, adjust and improve accordingly
Institutionalisation, structuring and integration	Principle 5: Embed engagement processes in clear legal and policy frameworks, organisational structures/principles and responsible authorities
Adaptiveness	Principle 6: Customise the type and level of engagement as needed and keep the process flexible to changing circumstances

Source: OECD (2015[14]), *Stakeholder Engagement for Inclusive Water Governance*, http://dx.doi.org/10.1787/9789264231122-en.

Box 2.3. Cape Town's strategy for building resilience through partnership and collaboration

The City of Cape Town recognises that collaborative relationships need to be built and maintained at many levels of the Cape Town water system, including between:

- citizens and city government
- customers and service providers
- citizens and political leadership
- officials and politicians
- City of Cape Town departments
- spheres of government
- businesses and the City of Cape Town
- the City of Cape Town and the scientific community
- the City of Cape Town and other users of the WCWSS.

Collaborative relationships are based on trust, and trust is built where there is transparency and mutual accountability, and where the stated intentions of all partners consistently translate into action. Based on the intensive experiences of engagement during the drought, the City of Cape Town will promote and facilitate building trust in tangible ways:

- **Engaging citizens and civil society.** The City of Cape Town will endeavour to create an enabling environment to be responsive to citizen-led water initiatives. The city will continue to work with social partners and collaborative intermediary organisations. It will undertake regular social surveys to better understand the needs and perceptions of citizens, and work with research institutions, NGOs and neighbourhood organisations that have established processes for documenting community water use and needs, perceptions and attitudes.

- **Engaging business.** The City of Cape Town will continue to work with collaborative intermediary organisations such as GreenCape, Wesgro and the WWF to better understand business needs and perceptions, and improve communication.
- **Engaging government.** The City of Cape Town will continue to work with collaborative intermediaries such as the Western Cape Economic Development Partnership (EDP) and the National Treasury's City of Cape Town Support Programme to facilitate productive relationships with other spheres of government, including the Western Cape Government and various national government departments.
- **Engaging labour.** The City of Cape Town will continue to work with organised labour as a key partner in service delivery to ensure that the rights of workers are protected.
- **Engaging researchers.** The City of Cape Town will continue to engage with research working groups such as the Freshwater Forum, the Cape Higher Education Consortium, the Water Research Group, the Water Research Commission and the Water Hub to develop and pursue applied research and evidence-based decision-making to assist the City of Cape Town to better fulfil its mandate and implement this strategy. The City of Cape Town will also explore a transdisciplinary research approach and partner with researchers to co-design research agendas and projects for the city.
- **Engaging key customers.** The City of Cape Town will set up a key-customers unit to be more responsive to their needs.
- **Engaging international expertise and experience.** The City of Cape Town will enhance existing and develop new knowledge-sharing partnerships with national and international bodies able to share relevant knowledge and experience to enable more effective implementation of this strategy. Where appropriate, Cape Town will make use of collaborative intermediates to support this effort. In addition, the City is committed to sharing its own experiences with these institutions to contribute to the global community of practice.

Source: OECD (2021[15]), *Water Governance in Cape Town, South Africa*, https://doi.org/10.1787/a804bd7b-en; City of Cape Town (2019[16]), *Cape Town Water Strategy*, https://resource.capetown.gov.za/documentcentre/Documents/City%20strategies%2c%20plans%20and%20frameworks.

Involvement of underserved/disadvantaged communities requires and is receiving more attention. However, water management professionals need to do more outreach, especially regarding the historical and ecological knowledge of native communities that are sovereign, have rights, but are generally poorly consulted (Box 2.4).

Box 2.4. The Fitzroy River Declaration for greater stakeholder engagement

In the Fitzroy River basin (Australia), the OECD Principles are providing a tool for under-represented stakeholders to promote their engagement in water policy design and implementation. An indigenous community from Australia developed a political declaration aiming to protect the traditional and environmental values that underpin the Fitzroy River's heritage. The aboriginal community has been the traditional guardian of the river for centuries, but increasing development in the watershed is jeopardising the future of the river and its people. The Fitzroy River Declaration, developed based on the OECD Principles, urges the government to set up a governance system in Western Australia that allows for greater stakeholder engagement and ultimately joint management of the river between the government and aboriginal communities.

Traditional Owners of the Kimberley region of Western Australia are concerned by the extensive development proposals facing the Fitzroy River and its catchment and the potential for cumulative impacts on its unique cultural and environmental values. The unique cultural and environmental values of the Fitzroy River and its catchment are of national and international significance. The Fitzroy River is a living ancestral being and has a right to life. It must be protected for current and future generations, and managed jointly by the Traditional Owners of the river.

Traditional Owners of the Fitzroy catchment agree to work together to:

1. Action a process for joint Prescribed Body Corporates decision making on activities in the Fitzroy catchment;
2. Reach a joint position on fracking in the Fitzroy catchment;
3. Create a buffer zone for no mining, oil, gas, irrigation and dams in the Fitzroy catchment;
4. Develop and agree a Management Plan for the entire Fitzroy Catchment, based on traditional and environmental values;
5. Develop a Fitzroy River Management Body for the Fitzroy Catchment, founded on cultural governance;
6. Complement these with a joint Indigenous Protected Area over the Fitzroy River;
7. Engage with shire and state government to communicate concerns and ensure they follow the agreed joint process;
8. Investigate legal options to support the above, including:
    a. Strengthen protections under the Environment Protection and Biodiversity Conservation Act National Heritage Listing;
    b. Strengthen protections under the Aboriginal Heritage Act; and
    c. Legislation to protect the Fitzroy catchment and its unique cultural and natural values.

Source: OECD (2018[13]), *Implementing the OECD Principles on Water Governance: Indicator Framework and Evolving Practices*, https://doi.org/10.1787/9789264292659-en; Martuwarra Fitzroy River (2016[17]), *Fitzroy River Declaration*, https://martuwarrafitzroyriver.org/fitzroy-river-declaration.

Communication methods and tools are crucial to strengthen the dynamics of collectively agreed water management agreements. In Arizona, communication practices have improved over the last few years. A few years ago, meetings held at Central Arizona Project headquarters in North Phoenix started to be broadcast so that more stakeholders could watch and observe. The pandemic accelerated and improved this trend with the introduction of interactive and remote meetings. Most meetings are held by public bodies, which must share agendas, announce meetings, provide access to materials/resources, etc. Leadership is making much more of an effort to travel and talk to people. Good memos also proved important to convey and share information. It is important to have an accurate database to provide clear, harmonised data and information. Databases are useful especially when dealing with groundwater because modelling highlights evolutions that are otherwise invisible. Stakeholders can be sceptical, and it is important to be transparent about the models used.

Investing in monitoring and hydrology control

Regarding water use compliance, the Annual Declaration of Water Use (DAURH) is an important self-reporting instrument that requires major Brazilian water users to report their annual water volume consumption. DAURH is required in basins and systems where there is pressure on water resources, and has improved the monitoring of water use in many river basins in Brazil. In the PPA river basin, it was required from users representing 75% of water demand met from the six major reservoirs. Other water use monitoring methodologies have been implemented, such as remote sensing of irrigated areas, water use data telemetry, and water use self-reporting using mobile apps. Moreover, the technical office contracted in 2016 executed several activities to support water use compliance assessment in both federal and state waters. Those activities included identification and registration of water users, flow measurement, monitoring of reservoir operations, identification of obstructions in rivers, and technical visits to dams. From 2017 to 2020, more than two thousand technical visits were carried out to check water use status and verify compliance with the rules of uses. In addition, satellite imagery has been used to remotely identify and monitor agricultural areas in the region, as well as irregular uses for which ANA coordinated removal of water pumps and the closure of irregular canals. The combination of field activities with intelligent remote technologies improved water use compliance and helped control water demand through the severe drought from 2013 to 2019. However, further improvements in the monitoring and assessment of water use across the basin are needed and under discussion. Such improvements include operational water management functions to support the implementation of the water allocation rules, like hydrologic and water demand monitoring and control, river dredging, reservoir operations, dam maintenance and safety, water use efficiency, and pollution control. Box 2.5 provides international examples.

Box 2.5. Monitoring and hydrological control in Spain, France and California, US

Conditioning water rights on control and reporting

In the Júcar River Basin (JRB), Spain, when a water right is granted, it is mandatory for the holder to install a control system and report information to the Commission of Users. Water right can even be removed from holder in case of non-reporting. Nevertheless, this control system requires an important enforcement capacity due to the 4 000 wells installed in the JRB. Efforts have been made to better control water withdrawal, especially in areas where groundwater is over exploited. In the South of the JRB, control is performed by people on the ground. In the Mancha Oriental, control is performed using tele-detection. Nevertheless, the EU is urging Spain to increase control over water withdrawal and use. More and more stakeholder engagement is also required to improve hydrological control and monitoring. Sanctions and penalties are also considered to improve compliance with control and monitoring. To enhance water use reporting and compliance in the PPA river basin, the DAURH obligation could be tied to the removal of water rights in the case of repeated non-reporting or inaccurate reporting. This could increase water use reporting and compliance while enhancing water resource monitoring and water allocation enforcement. Nevertheless, sanctions should be preceded and supported by intensive stakeholder engagement processes.

More stringent assessment and management in areas of water stress

In France, water is generally abundant, although water stress is increasing in some regions and there are periodic episodes of scarcity. In areas of water stress, more detailed assessments of water availability and use are required. Laws related to management of water resources are stricter in these areas and the allocation regime is more rigorous. A mapping exercise has been undertaken to identify ground and surface water stressed areas. This is used to define water apportionment areas, where the water deficit is structural. These zones are the target of recent reforms to restore sustainable abstractable volumes as well as the creation of Single Collective Management Bodies (Organismes Uniques de Gestion Collective, OUGC) to provide an incentive for irrigators to allocate a set volume of water among themselves at catchment level.

Hydrology models to foster dialogue and support decision-making

Hydrology models are not only important tools to allocate water resources, they are also useful to foster dialogue among water stakeholders, and support informed decision-making. As such, they should be used early on. In California, hydrology modelling proved useful to provide a better understanding of the hydrological situation and its likely evolution, thus helping to make better decisions. Data accuracy problems can be important, underlining the need for a common and harmonised accounting system throughout a river basin. Models can also be useful to improve data. Based on the experience of California, it is recommended to build and use hydrology models early, and improve them along the way rather than collecting data for years before starting to build a model. In Spain, the evaluation of available resources and demands in each water resource system are carried out in the River Basin Management Plans. An inventory of available water resources is produced, and existing water uses and demands are identified. Water resource assessment methods have been developed for the whole national territory, as well as simulation water resource models that take into account conventional and non-conventional water resources, environmental flows, water demands, hydraulic infrastructure, water use priorities, and exploitation rules in order to establish water allocations and reserves.

Source: OECD/ANA (2021[18]), "Workshop on Strengthening River Basin Governance in the Piancó-Piranhas Açu River Basin (25-28 May 2021)".

Improving water allocation mechanisms

The term "water allocation regime" is used to describe the process and tools involved in sharing water resources amongst different water users. This includes establishing water resource plans that define the availability of water and granting water permits to individual water users. It also includes allocating water resources over the long term, as well as seasonal adjustments to the amount of water available to different users, and the allocation of both surface water and groundwater. Several tools exist for translating allocation principles into concrete water management. They include water management plans, water permits, collective entitlements, and enforcement and monitoring tools.

OECD (2015[19]), shows that Brazil made remarkable progress in reforming its water sector since the National Water Law of 1997. However, economic, climatic and urbanisation drivers can increase tensions between water users in some regions and basins, such as the Piancó-Piranhas-Açu (PPA) river basin. The report recommends strengthening coordination between federal and state water policies and putting in place more robust water allocation regimes that can better cope with future risks of water shortage (Box 2.6).

Box 2.6. 2015 OECD assessment and recommendations for water allocation in Brazil

Three major weaknesses must be addressed

Water resources plans – at the federal, interstate, and relevant state, river basin or hydrological planning unit level – do not set priorities or criteria that can drive allocation decisions. Moreover, plans generally do not include cyclical events such as droughts and thus lack clarity in terms of priority of water use in times of crisis. Sectoral planning occurs largely in isolation (e.g., hydropower development, irrigation extension), frequently unconnected to the water resource planning process.

Responsibility for many allocation decisions is with river basin committees or state agencies – entities whose water allocation priorities may differ from those at the federal level. Potential tensions between federal and state priorities are exacerbated by challenges related to the "double dominion": for rivers in the Union domain, the Constitution confers the criteria for granting permits for water withdrawal to the federal level (ANA) from the main channel, and to the states from the tributaries.

Implementation of water allocation policy remains the exception rather than the rule.

Suggestions for robust water allocation regimes in Brazil

A combination of three sets of measures can help address the identified weaknesses.

First, available water resources and the priorities for water use must be clearly defined:

- Define reference flows that maximise the benefits and efficiency of water use; this could involve water use rights with different levels of reliability or allowing users to determine their own levels of risk.
- Water resource plans must identify priorities and guide allocation decisions; plans should encourage the multi-purpose use of water from reservoirs.

Second, policy instruments must be designed to serve the objectives of the water allocation policy:

- Define criteria for issuing water use permits that are consistent and increase flexibility for water users (e.g., collective rights to use irrigation water).
- Design economic instruments that combine efficiency and flexibility, including pricing instruments to facilitate the reallocation of water between water users.

Third, define governance arrangements to ensure efficient allocation:

- Set up mechanisms for monitoring and enforcing the water allocation regime.
- Make institutional arrangements to strengthen the capacity of states to develop plans and define priorities, including coherence with the federal level for dual dominion watercourses.
- Inform, build capacities and involve water users in decision-making.

Source: OECD (2015[19]), *Water Resources Governance in Brazil*, https://doi.org/10.1787/9789264238121-en.

All of Brazil's water resources are in the public domain (federal or state). The National Water Act of 1997 stipulates that human consumption and livestock have priority over other uses in periods of water scarcity. Pursuant to Decree 3.692/2000, ANA should set minimum flows for state rivers that feed into federal rivers.

Depending on the estimated water supply/demand balance for the coming year, reservoirs and rivers can be subject to negotiated water allocations for that year (Alocação de Água, AA). A permanent water resource compact (Marco Regulatório, MR) is established for reservoirs and rivers with a chronic water deficit (having been the subject of several AAs). The aim is to set limits on the total volume of water available for allocation and establish rules for sharing water during periods of scarcity. Both instruments generally set out:

- a quota for each use of water (human water supply, irrigation, etc.)
- water use restrictions to preserve multiple uses in the event of water scarcity

Water allocation regimes in the PPA river basin were established through water agreements at local level. In 2018 and 2019, after an intensive discussion process, new MRs were discussed and implemented for the major reservoir systems of the river basin. In many cases, water allocation rules evolved into joint resolutions signed by ANA and state government agencies defining water use rule for both federal and state waters, thus addressing issues related to the double dominion. Such water allocation agreements usually establish a quota for each water use, considering water availability from the hydrologic system. There are also water use restriction rules associated with reservoir levels or river stream flows. However, further institutional development is needed to implement water allocation rules, both in local water systems and large river reaches.

Implementation of AAs and MRs in the PPA basin started in 2015. In 2021, seven (out of eleven) reservoirs located in the basin were under MR and two more are subject to an AA. In addition to AAs and MRs, compliance with the minimum levels of river flows and water in reservoirs set by the Water Act 1997 may lead to further restrictions on water use.

CBH leads the AA process. Ad hoc commissions ensure the proper implementation of the AAs and communicate on the state of water resources and the risks of water scarcity. MRs are enforceable by way of a resolution made by either the ANA or the relevant state water agency, or both. They comprise sets of rules defined in consultation with local governments and water users (e.g. reference flows at various points throughout the basin, as a basis for allocation decisions). Where they are in force, any water permits must include conditions requiring the water user to comply with the rules set by the MR.

Table 2.2 summarises the key features of Brazil's water allocation regime.

Table 2.2. Brazil's water allocation regime

Components	Feature
Legal context for water allocation	Roman law as opposed to common law (in force in Australia and the United States), i.e., there are no riparian rights or prior appropriation in Brazil, but statutory water use rights unbundled from land property titles
Allocation priority	By law, human consumption and livestock have priority over water allocation in drought conditions; at the basin level, the order of priority between the other uses of water can be fixed by statute by the river basin plan or implicitly by the water resources compact
	By law, the energy guaranteed from hydropower can only vary by 5% every five years and by 10% during the 35 years of concession
	Environmental flows are defined by environmental agencies and vary according to the river
Water entitlement	Cannot be traded or leased, but can be transferred
	Can be lost if not used for 3 years
	Individual permits are not differentiated based on the level of security of supply (or risk of shortage)
	Granted for 10 years (small irrigated area; small industries; aquaculture; livestock farms; mining; others); 20 years (irrigated areas above 2 000 ha; industries withdrawing above 1 m³/s) or 35 years (reservoirs for flood control or hydropower and other hydraulic structures; public water supply and sanitation); states may have their own rules defining how long entitlements are valid
	In selected federal rivers, users with water abstraction above defined limits are obliged to install measuring devices
	Entitlement requests are subject to an impact assessment on existing water entitlements; in specific situations established by law, new requests for entitlements can motivate new water resources compacts which can lead to revising current entitlements
Abstraction limits	At the basin level, the water resources compact sets permanent abstraction limits/quotas for each consumptive use of water (e.g., maximum irrigated area of 'x' hectares corresponding to a cap of 'y' m³/s)
	At the level of the water body, in the event of shortage, the allocation can be lower than the entitlement and vary from year to year and season to season depending on discussions with water users ("negotiated water allocation")
Abstraction charges	Water entitlement holders can be required to pay a charge for water withdrawal from basins where those charges are established, such as São Francisco River basin; based on the annual volume of water withdrawn (counted or declared) for agriculture, industry and households; based on energy production

	(6.75%) for hydropower
Conflict resolution mechanism	Water conflicts are first brought to the CBH for resolution; if not resolved, the conflict can be brought to the attention of CERHS or CNRH; conflicts between CERHs are resolved by the CNRH

Source: Adapted from OECD (2015[20]), *Water Resources Allocation: Sharing Risks and Opportunities*, https://doi.org/10.1787/9789264229631-en.

However, the National Water Resources Policy (PNRH) does not provide clear guidance on how water allocation between sectors should be resolved in times of water scarcity. To manage the risk of scarcity, water allocation in the PPA basin is based mainly on agreements negotiated between users on an annual basis (AAs), which can turn into statutory regulation (MR) if the risk of water shortage in a river or reservoir persists.

Pricing instruments can allocate water among users more cost-effectively. This is the case with abstraction charges provided for in the National Water Law of 1997, as introduced to some extent in the state of Paraiba, provided that they reflect the risk of scarcity and that the rates are not differentiated between users. Cap-and-trade systems would be the most cost-effective by setting (1) an abstraction cap and (2) a price for the water permit, implicitly taxing the abstraction according to the water demand, thus improving water use efficiency. Abstraction charges and cap-and-trade systems (water markets) are discussed below, as well as the combination between them or with direct regulation.

Environmental Flows

Water allocation is, in essence, a means to manage the risk of shortage and to adjudicate between competing uses. When setting up water allocation regimes, reference flows should involve consideration of non-consumptive water demands, including environmental flows (e-flows), which indicate the flow regime required to sustain ecosystem services at the required level (Box 2.7).

Box 2.7. Options for treatment of in-stream flows within a water allocation regime

When designing an allocation regime and setting a long-term abstraction limit, it is important to decide whether to include some or all entitlements in this limit. The most common approach is to set aside the amount needed for environmental needs, non-consumptive uses, and transfers to other systems (including downstream obligations) as a prior right, then allocate the remainder for consumptive uses.

An alternative approach being tested in Australia is to assign some water to the environment as an entitlement to a share of all inflows and define this entitlement separately from the arrangements used to ensure that base flows, for example, are maintained. In the Murray-Darling Basin, a Commonwealth Environmental Water Holder was established and is expected to hold around one third of the basin's water entitlements by 2019. Under this arrangement, the government cannot allocate water to consumptive users without a pro rata allocation to the Commonwealth Environmental Water Holder.

Australia is using this approach to put environmental water on the same footing as all other water users. Under this arrangement, allocations are made in proportion to the number of entitlements held in the interests of the environment, no matter how dry or wet it is. As a result, administrators are not able to transfer environmental water to other users.

In the United States, non-governmental groups have been buying water to ensure that the environment is looked after. A well-known example is the Oregon Water Trust, which became a programme of The Freshwater Trust in 2008.

Source: OECD (2015[20]), *Water Resources Allocation: Sharing Risks and Opportunities*, https://doi.org/10.1787/9789264229631-en.

Environmental flow is a very technical subject (with minimum rate, maximum rate, rate of flow over time). A large piece of the environmental flow determination focuses on minimum water flows in relation to water scarcity, with the objective to preserve ecosystems downstream (Box 2.7). Different methodologies can be used. One is based on historical data which are used to analyse historical minimum flows. Through historical data modelling, a minimum flow regulation is determined. Another method is using biological studies to determine the preferences of fish and the associated minimum flow requirements. This method is performed with the support of academics and researchers from universities. In addition, there is important hydrological work and planning done with electricity suppliers to adapt the flows.

In Spain, the vision of environmental requirements has changed a lot. In the past, the dominant vision was very much utilitarian with the purpose of using water and environment to create wealth. The focus started to change in the 1990s when an important drought compromised urban water provision. Later, the Water Framework Directive helped develop and strengthen the concept of ecological flow of rivers. There is still a need to increase these flows but it is sometimes difficult to make users understand that maintaining some ecological conditions is necessary. This will become more and more important in the future, especially to adapt to climate change with increasing water temperature becoming a problem. The importance of environmental flows is now widely recognised, and failure to provide adequate environmental flows can lead to a wide range of negative, and often unexpected, impacts (Box 2.8).

> **Box 2.8. Impacts of failing to consider environmental flows**
>
> Freshwater systems provide a wide range of ecosystem services. Changes to the natural flow regime can impact the ability of a river to provide these. Poor water allocation practices can mean that many of the services that rivers provide – for free – can be lost, with significant impact on dependent human communities. Examples from international experience include:
>
> - **Heightened flood risk**, such as in China's Yellow River, where over-allocation resulted in the build-up of sediment and changes to river morphology. This led to the river being perched above the floodplain and a significant increase in the risk of flooding. Dedicated flows representing around 35% of the mean annual flow are now provided in the allocation regime to improve sediment movement as part of efforts to reduce the risk of flooding.
> - **Saltwater encroachment and related environmental declines**, such as in Pakistan's Indus River, where over-allocation and massively reduced flows at the river mouth led to saltwater intruding 64 kilometres inland and the loss of approximately 1.2 million acres of farmland.
> - **Declines in fish and other aquatic populations**, such as in China's Yangtze River, where changes to the downstream flow regime because of construction of the Three Gorges Dam caused a decline of up to 95% in juvenile fish stocks of the four major carp species, with subsequent effects on fisheries production.
>
> Source: Poff, L., R. Tharme and A. Arthington (2017[21]), "Evolution of environmental flows assessment science, principles, and methodologies", http://dx.doi.org/10.1016/B978-0-12-803907-6.00011-5.

In the US, environmental needs and demands for water are decentralised and vary across jurisdictions. Dealing with environmental flow is key to keep the aquatic ecosystems in good state as this increases sustainability and improves water quality. Nevertheless, environmental flows and needs are hard to value.

Compensation mechanisms

The priority given by law to human consumption and livestock over other uses in times of water scarcity can lead (and has) to depriving farmers of their acquired rights to water, with economic consequences due to the absence of a financial compensation mechanism. To compensate farmers faced with this situation, or to prevent this situation from occurring, three options could be considered: (1) a federally guaranteed insurance or reinsurance scheme could be combined with the current AA/MR quota scheme, (2) the generalisation of abstraction charges could replace direct regulation (i.e., the AA/RM regime) with a system of cross-subsidisation in favour of farmers as described above, or (3) auctioning of AA/MR quotas could be allowed, but grandfathering the original rights of farmers.

In Brazil, the large public banks (Banco do Brasil, Banco de Amazonia) cover crop insurance premiums (to an extent) for poor farmers. There is no irrigation insurance. It is indeed more cost-effective to cover the risk of non-production instead of covering the risk of lack of irrigation water. The latter could be considered as a subsidy of agricultural inputs and fall under the subsidy discipline of the WTO.

Multi-risk insurance (pests, droughts, damage caused by wildlife to crops, etc.) would increase the basis for insurance premiums and reduce the rate. The same reasoning applies to insurance at the basin level to pool the risk between all the farmers in the basin. Multi-year insurance contracts would allow better recovery of premiums (by spreading the risk). Defining a drought risk threshold (an "acceptable" level of drought risk) would improve transparency in setting insurance premiums.

To avoid moral hazard, instead of subsidising the insurance premium of some (poor) farmers, it would be more cost-effective to apply a floor premium for all farmers, introduce an additional premium for the rich and redistribute income to the poorest to help them pay the floor premium.

Water pricing instruments could usefully complement crop insurance. In the event of drought, water markets compensate (in part) for the loss of agricultural production with a higher value of water rights, especially long-term entitlements (market adjustment). The generalisation of abstraction charges according to the risk of scarcity would require setting an acceptable scarcity risk threshold, thus improving the implementation of crop insurance. Box 2.9 provides an overview of the functioning of agricultural risk management instruments in OECD countries and emerging economies.

Box 2.9. Agricultural risk management instruments

A key role of government in agricultural risk management (ARM) is to facilitate the development of information about agricultural risks. Better ex ante risk assessment reduces adverse selection problems that arise because producers know more than insurers about the risks affecting their crop production.

Government support for ARM policies should be limited to providing protection against "catastrophic losses", defined by the WTO as losses exceeding 30% of historical average production or income level. However, since the launch of agricultural policy reforms in the late 1980s aimed at phasing out border protection and guaranteed producer prices, governments of OECD countries and emerging economies nearly quadrupled spending on ARM policies, reaching USD 25 billion in 2019. This includes agricultural insurance (73% of spending in 2019), ex post disaster aid (20%), income stabilisation schemes (5%), and tax and savings measures (2%).

Agricultural insurance guarantees producers a level of yield or revenue in exchange for a premium paid based on an actuarial estimate of risk. It can offer protection against a single peril (such as crop insurance) or multiple perils. Claims are based on either actual loss of yield (indemnity-based contracts) or regional yield, weather or other variables (index-based contracts).

Ex post disaster aid compensates producers after a natural disaster. Most often, the decision by the government whether to intervene is taken after the fact, so that at the time of planting, producers do not know whether they will be protected in the event of a disaster.

> **Income stabilisation schemes** aim to keep producers' income around the average of recent years, generally guaranteeing a minimum income. Unlike agricultural insurance, which targets individual crops, income stabilisation concerns the entire farm.
>
> **Tax and savings measures** aim to smooth income variability through tax-deferred savings accounts where the government matches producer savings deposits up to a set amount and allows producers to opt out of the programme, often without penalty, in years when farm income falls below a set level.
>
> Government spending on ARM policies can represent a significant share of producer support (PSE), estimated by the OECD as a % of gross farm receipts. In 2017-19, they accounted for 15% of PSE in Brazil, 22% in the United States, 30% in Canada and 50% in Australia, but only 3% in the EU-28.
>
> ARM policies (agricultural insurance) distort production choices and the use of farm inputs, including irrigation water, and are therefore more likely to increase environmental pressure than ARM policies supporting income (income stabilisation schemes, tax and savings measures). The most effective way to manage the risk of irrigation water scarcity through income-supporting ARM policies would be to make the subsidy of insurance premiums conditional on environmental outcomes, such as the efficiency of irrigation water use.
>
> A problem common to all ARM policies is that they create moral hazards – an insured has incentive to increase his exposure to risk because he does not bear the full costs of that risk. To minimise moral hazard, most ARM policies have either a deductible (i.e., the producer must pay for losses up to an agreed level at which the insurance begins to cover) and/or a co-payment where the insurer pays only part of the indemnity (the rest being absorbed by the insured). For example, under the United States crop insurance program, deductibles are often set at 25% or more for crops where actuarial experience may be limited
>
> Source: Glauber, J. et al. (2021[22]), "Design principles for agricultural risk management policies", https://doi.org/10.1787/1048819f-en.

International experience shows that information and stakeholder engagement are key to resolving conflicts in the absence of compensation mechanisms. In California, the role of the state is to create a common water accounting system so that all stakeholders have access to and use similar data and information. Having data and a common basis for technical understanding is crucial for agreement over time. State or local governments can then organise discussions on water allocation using the information from the water accounting system. This is commonly done in California around the issue of water rights. Discussions occur locally before the drought, as the pressure of emergency during the drought increases political sensitivity. Most water decisions are made locally where water demand lies and where land-use and other water demand drivers occur. In addition, this brings more direct accountability and power to water users. In Spain, urban water supply is considered a priority water use. Hence, there is normally no compensation of other users when water use is restricted or cut in case of droughts. However, during the 2005-2006 drought, a public offer was made to sell rights to groundwater use to maintain ecological flow. This successfully reduced pumping. Furthermore, in the Spanish Mediterranean coast, traditional tribunals are in charge of settling water use conflicts between irrigators (Box 2.10).

> ### Box 2.10. Irrigators' tribunals on the Spanish Mediterranean coast
>
> The irrigators' tribunals on the Spanish Mediterranean coast are traditional law courts for water management that date back to the Al-Andalus period (9th to 13th Centuries). The two main tribunals – the Council of Wise Men of the Plain of Murcia and the Water Tribunal of the Plain of Valencia – are recognised under Spanish law. Inspiring authority and respect, these two courts, whose members are

> elected democratically, settle disputes orally in a swift, transparent and impartial manner. The Council of Wise Men has seven geographically representative members and jurisdiction over a landowners' assembly of 23 313 members. The Water Tribunal comprises eight elected administrators representing a total of 11 691 members from nine communities. In addition to their legal role, the irrigators' tribunals are a key part of the communities of which they are a visible symbol, as apparent from the rites performed when judgments are handed down and the fact that the tribunals often feature in local iconography. They provide cohesion among traditional communities and synergy between occupations (wardens, inspectors, pruners, etc.), contribute to the oral transmission of knowledge derived from centuries-old cultural exchanges, and have their own specialist vocabulary peppered with Arabic borrowings. In short, the courts are long-standing repositories of local and regional identity and are of special significance to local inhabitants.
>
> The Court of Waters of the valley of Valencia (*Tribunal de las Aguas de la Vega de Valencia*), is an institution of justice in charge of settling disputes arising from the use of irrigation water among farmers. It is the oldest existing institution of justice in Europe. The Court of Waters is a customary court made up of a representative from each of the eight Irrigation Communities, called Trustees. The Court President is elected among these Irrigation Communities for a renewable period of two years. Every Thursday of the week, the Court meets in a public session in the afternoon while an administrative session is held later in the day to discuss various matters, mainly the distribution of water.
>
> Source: UNESCO (2021[23]), "Irrigators' tribunals of the Spanish Mediterranean coast: the Council of Wise Men of the plain of Murcia and the Water Tribunal of the plain of Valencia", https://ich.unesco.org/en/RL/irrigators-tribunals-of-the-spanish-mediterranean-coast-the-council-of-wise-men-of-the-plain-of-murcia-and-the-water-tribunal-of-the-plain-of-valencia-00171.

Strengthening economic instruments in the Piancó-Piranhas Açu river basin

Pricing and financing of integrated water resources management in the PPA basin

Three major economic challenges arise in the PPA basin. The first is O&M funding for bulk water storage and transport infrastructure, which is critical to this semi-arid area. It is even more important given that the inter-basin transfer of the São Francisco River raises hopes for socio-economic development in the basin. The PPA basin is sorely lacking in money for O&M of the basin's small reservoirs. There is seemingly no provision to cover the O&M of these infrastructures in the pricing of water and sanitation or irrigation water services. The second challenge is the implementation of the principle of water pays for water, consisting of allocating the proceeds of abstraction charges to IWRM (to CBH). The third challenge is water allocation and demand management to promote efficient water use and cost-effectively manage the risk of scarcity.

Pricing instruments (water charges, water markets) are relevant to address the three challenges. They create incentives to reduce water demand and allocate water costs effectively. They collect funds to finance infrastructure and integrated water resources management (IWRM). A conceptual framework is proposed to set up pricing and financing instruments in the PPA basin (Figure 2.6). User charges (known in Brazil as "serviço de adução de água bruta") and abstraction charges (known in Brazil as "cobrança", as stated in the National Water Law of 1997) have different objectives. The first aims to recover the costs of water supply services (requited payment). The latter aims to manage water resources and should contribute to the general budget (unrequited payment). Although limiting flexibility in the use of public funds, but improving the public/political acceptability of abstraction charges, the application of the principle of water pays for water. The principle could also apply in the case of a cap-and-trade system of water use rights at auction, by allocating the proceeds of the auction to IWRM.

Bulk users must finance the O&M of storage and transport infrastructure (reservoirs and PISF) via user charges (*serviço de adução de água bruta*), according to the very definition of user charges (payment in return for services) (Figure 2.6). User charges can be passed on to the water bill of end users (i.e., water tariffs). As a rule of thumb, as with urban water supply infrastructure, any recourse to public funding for the O&M of bulk water infrastructure should be considered temporary, with user charges eventually recovering all costs to ensure the financial sustainability of infrastructure operators.

Figure 2.6. Conceptual framework for the pricing and financing of integrated water resources management in the PPA basin

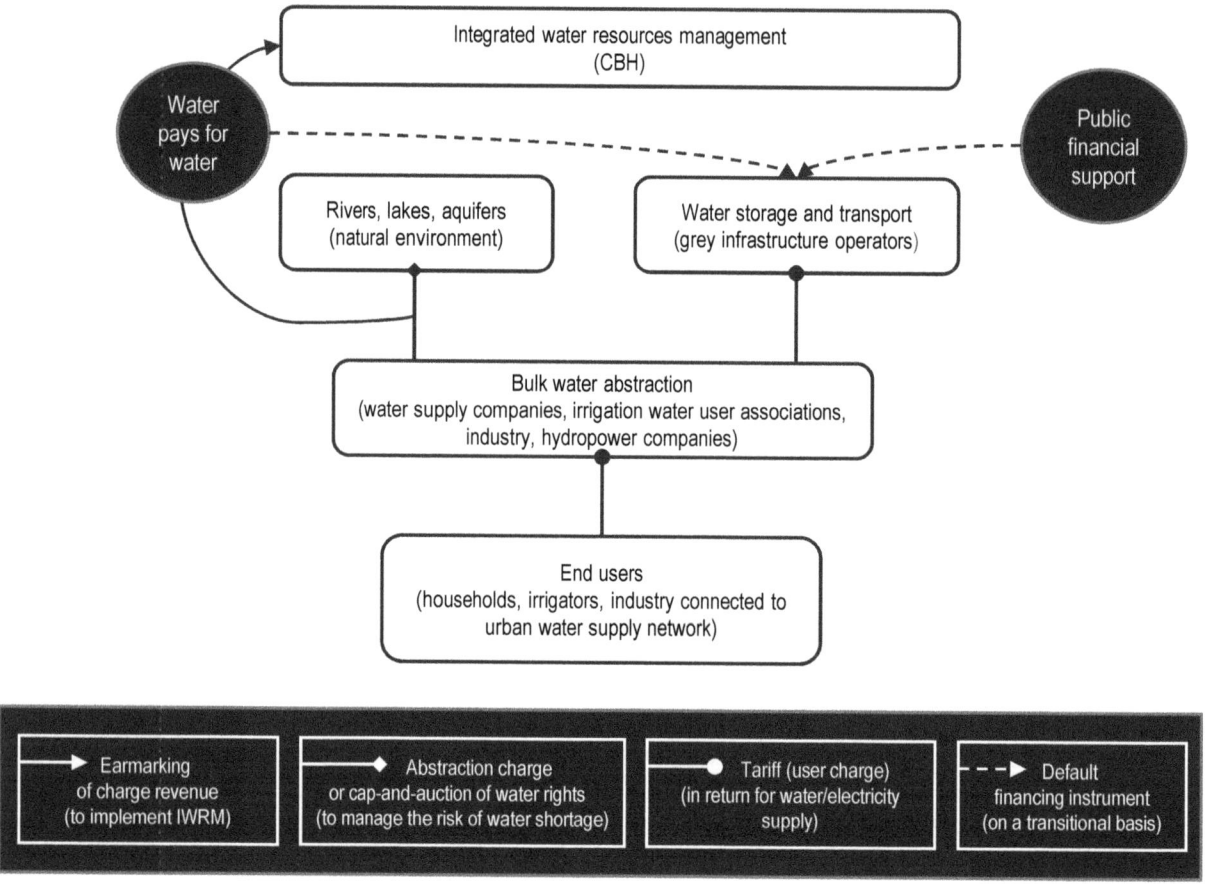

Financing the operation and maintenance of water storage and transport infrastructure

Financing the O&M of large water storage and transport infrastructure (bulk water) is essential for the security of water supply in the PPA basin. The federal government bears the capital costs of all major federal bulk water infrastructure projects but is not expected to bear the O&M costs. In practice, however, payments from state water agencies (AESA and IGARN) to the operator of federal reservoirs (DNOCS) for bulk water only cover a portion of the O&M costs of federal reservoirs. DNOCS (that is, the federal public treasury) fills the gap. The Ministry of Regional Development (MDR) recently submitted a bill to Congress to require users to cover the costs of operating and maintaining federal reservoirs.

The same principle should apply to cover the O&M costs of the PISF as it goes into service. In other words, water users in the four states served by PISF (Ceará, Paraíba, Pernambuco and Rio Grande do Norte) should pay its federal operator (CODEVASF) enough to fully fund O&M. ANA (as regulator of water supply and sanitation since 2020) plans to revise the user charge structure to allow the recovery of the O&M costs of the PISF (estimated at USD 53 million per year for the four states served by the PISF). The new structure would consist of two components: a standing charge (USD $0.05/m^3$) to cover the fixed costs of O&M of the PISF and an additional volumetric charge (USD $0.09/m^3$) to recover the cost of pumping water from the PISF (mainly electricity costs). The same structure and charge rates would apply to the four states served by PISF. Financing of the O&M of other bulk water infrastructure (non-federal) is at the discretion of state water policy.

The lack of an explicit policy on cost recovery for the O&M of bulk water supply infrastructure threatens the sustainability of the bulk water supply. A simple solution is that wholesale water users pay the full cost of operating and maintaining the wholesale water supply infrastructure. In other words, AESA, IGARN and any other large water users (e.g., cities, irrigation associations) should pay a user charge to CODEVASF and DNOCS covering the costs of O&M of reservoirs and PISF. Likewise, for non-federal bulk water supply infrastructure, O&M costs should be fully recovered from users. In addition, user charges create an incentive to reduce water consumption (improve water use efficiency), encouraging behaviour change.

All large water users should share O&M costs equally (similar volumetric rates for all) to improve feasibility (e.g., public acceptability) and send the same water conservation signal to all. To maintain the conservation signal for all, any cross-subsidy between bulk water sectors (e.g., between cities and irrigation associations) should be sought separately, for example by introducing an additional levy on the user charge of cities whose revenues would be redistributed to irrigation associations.

Public financial support for collective irrigated perimeters amounts to subsidising the costs of providing water for irrigation in agricultural production, which is subject to the subsidy discipline of the World Trade Organization (WTO) (Kibel, 2014[24]). It distorts water use by encouraging irrigation at the expense of other water uses. Managing irrigation water resources would be more cost-effective by directing public money to direct payments that help farmers purchase on-farm water-saving technologies (e.g., drip irrigation).

An argument in favour of public financing for the O&M of storage and transport the infrastructures for bulk water is their public benefits, such regulation of the flow of rivers, supplement of water to natural environments, etc. Debate over the impacts and benefits of bulk water supply infrastructure should be documented with technical and scientific arguments to inform policy making. If such public benefits are demonstrated, this could justify the coverage of O&M costs by the CBH, as part of its role as IWRM authority for the PPA basin. This involves financing the CBH by allocating revenue from abstraction charges in accordance with the principle of water pays for water implemented in Brazil. In France, for example, in 2021, the Adour-Garonne water agency earmarked EUR 4 million to support local communities in bringing their dams into compliance with the objective of "restoring the volumes initially available and improving their management for the benefit of natural environments". Typically, the CBH could provide financial assistance for O&M if the infrastructure has an environmental benefit and not just an economic benefit. By enhancing their environmental benefits, the "greening" of bulk water infrastructure (for example by seeking biodiversity or climate co-benefits with the planting of trees along canals or upstream of reservoirs) would increase eligibility for CBH support.

Making more room for green water infrastructure would allow the beneficiary-pays principle to be applied. This would involve asking the beneficiaries (cities, economic activities) of the PPA basin to remunerate the services of regulating the flow of rivers provided by ecosystems. The CBH could still provide financial assistance to O&M of green water infrastructure (e.g., wetlands, floodplains, alluvial forests) as they provide environmental benefits. The U.S. Army Corps of Engineers created *Engineering with Nature: An Atlas*, a compilation of 118 constructed projects around the world that show the benefits and diversity of nature-based solutions and how they can be implemented.

Floating solar panels are developing rapidly and massively in the PPA basin (in the state of Paraiba), impacting water resources. Possible effects of covering a reservoir with floating solar panels include, but are not limited to: reduced mixing by wind of the reservoirs, and changes in flora, fauna and related organisms (birds, fish, aquatic plants, mussels, insects, algae, bacteria, viruses, etc.) present in or around the reservoir (Mathijssen et al., 2020[25]). The solar panel operator should provide financial compensation to the water infrastructure operator for side effects on aquatic life and water quality. The amount of compensation should be used to protect and restore aquatic life and water quality. However, part could be allocated to financing the O&M of bulk water infrastructure, which would amount to applying a kind of "electricity pays for water" principle.

Even if it has been used mainly to promote urban development (the "city pays for the city" principle), value capture could be considered as a tool for financing bulk water infrastructure (Inter-American Development Bank, 2016[26]). In other words, the increase in the value of land served by bulk water infrastructure could be taxed over a specified period and the tax proceeds allocated to the O&M of such infrastructure (principle of "land pays for water"). Brazil has a tax system linked to the value of land, both in urban areas (Building and Urban Territorial Tax, IPTU) and in rural areas (Rural Territorial Tax, ITR). These taxes can partially capture the increase in land and property value resulting from the building of water infrastructure. However, the allocation of revenue is not earmarked and depends on the local executive. The collection competence is municipal (IPTU) and federal delegated to municipalities (ITR).

All these sources of financing could be mobilised to facilitate the transition to full recovery of O&M costs through bulk user charges and, for green infrastructure, payments for ecosystem services (Figure 2.7).

Figure 2.7. Financing O&M of bulk water infrastructure in the PPA basin

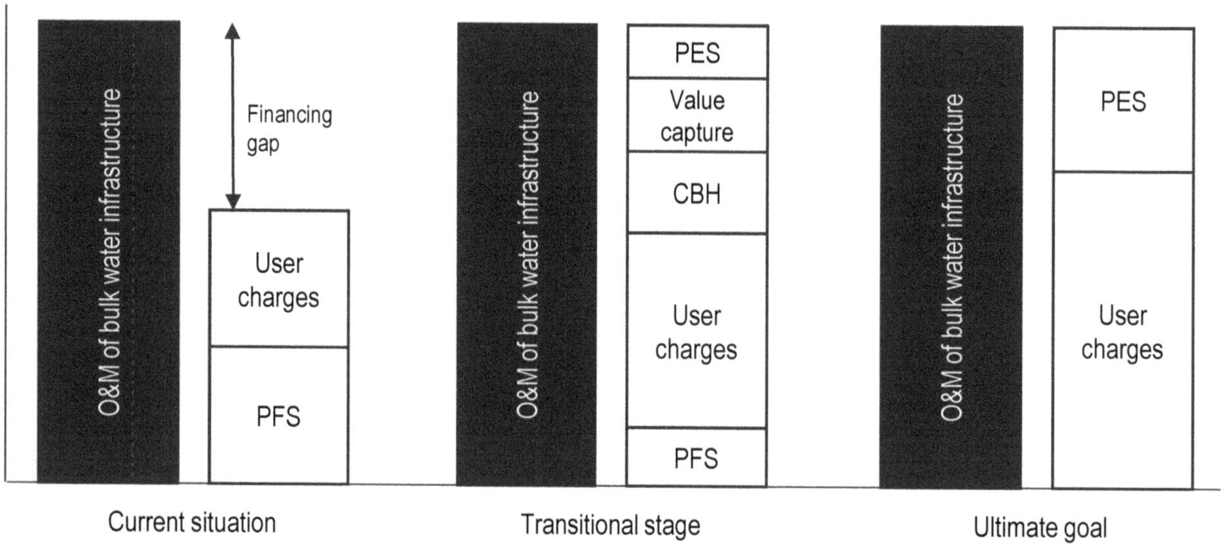

Notes: Bulk water infrastructure = reservoirs and PISF; PFS = public financial support (federal, state); User charges = charges for bulk water supply; CBH = PPA River Basin Committee (part of the revenue from abstraction charges); Value capture = tax on the price increase of land served by bulk hydraulic infrastructure; PES = payment for ecosystem services (applies to green infrastructure).

Financing the O&M of bulk water supply infrastructure through user charges applied to large water users, as required by the "principle of user-pays", raises the issue of water pricing for the end users to whom these charges will be passed. Tariffs alone should be sufficient to recover the costs of operating and maintaining retail water infrastructure. Relying on the public budget to supplement tariff revenues would make it easier to obtain repayable aid (loans, bonds, shares). However, this "sustainable cost recovery" approach should be seen as an intermediate step towards the ultimate goal of "full cost recovery" (Cox and Börkey, 2015[27]).

The 2006 agreement (*Termo de Compromisso*) between the Federal and States Government established that the States would cover the PISF operational and maintenance costs. While the States agreed to establish water tariffs, the agreement does not specify that only households would pay. Two States in the PISF region (Ceará and Paraíba) already charge for water use and that affects all sectors including irrigation. Nevertheless, revenues are not enough to cover PISF O&M costs. Beyond the PISF case, irrigators in collective, public irrigated districts can pay a water tariffs to cover irrigation O&M costs. In those cases, water tariffs are an obligation set by the irrigation district operator, the public company CODEVASF, but they would not cover the additional costs related to PISF.

By setting a low-rate consumption cap, increasing block tariffs (IBT) send a stronger conservation signal than simple volumetric tariffs, but they entail higher administrative costs. User charges that cover the full costs of operating and maintaining bulk water (reservoirs and PISF) will increase the water bill for end users. Affordability issues need to be addressed. Social pricing of retail water could be considered by differentiating volumetric tariff or first block size (cheap block), or both, with lower tariff/larger block size for poorer households (e.g. those who have access to social benefits). The water conservation signal would however be better preserved by setting the same volumetric tariff/block size for all, but adding an additional levy on the water bill of the rich and redistributing the income to the poorest to help them pay the water bill (cross subsidy between rich and poor). The same reasoning applies to irrigators.

The low standard of living (in GDP per capita) in the PPA basin should not be an obstacle to recovering the costs of operating and maintaining bulk water infrastructure through user charges (and ultimately, water bills) considering the benefits of a well-maintained water infrastructure on the well-being of the population of the basin, such as increased irrigated area or productivity gains from improved health. The risk of power outage that Brazil has experienced in past years due to insufficient water levels in hydropower dams should sensitise stakeholders in the PPA basin to the need to ensure adequate O&M for bulk water infrastructure in the basin.

Implementing the principle of water pays for water

The principle of water pays for water consists of allocating the proceeds of abstraction charges collected in the PPA basin to PPA basin management. OECD (2017[28]) assesses the system of water abstraction charges in Brazil and suggests possible improvements (Box 2.11). OECD (2017[28]) also provides a checklist to help Brazil implement water charges (Box 2.12).

Box 2.11. 2017 OECD assessment and recommendations on water abstraction charges in Brazil

The state of play of water charges in Brazil

Five interstate river basins (federal waters) and six states (state waters) implement water charges (*cobrança*), including the state of Paraíba since 2015. The PPA river basin and the state of Rio Grande do Norte are only beginning to discuss the feasibility of water charges.

However, experience with abstraction charges suffers from several limitations:

First, charges are too low and not designed to influence the behaviour of water users.

Second, the existing charges do not consider the risk of scarcity or drought at the local level - their structure and level are similar across the country - nor do they reflect the opportunity costs of water use in the basin where they are levied.

Third, the charge rate is designed primarily to criteria of affordability and competitiveness, which should be better assessed and not hinder the incentive to address the risk of scarcity or drought.

Fourth, the setting of the charge rate by river basin committees creates tensions between government and users, and makes any rate increase difficult. Decision-making based on the individual risks of users would help manage trade-offs between stakeholders in the basin and make better use of charge revenues (based on a risk-benefit analysis of the projects proposed for the basin).

Ways forward

Charges should be designed to reduce water risks in the basin where they are levied and provide visible benefits to increase the willingness to pay of users. Pragmatically, the priority at first could be to target those with the largest water withdrawals to maximise the benefits in terms of managing the risk of scarcity and raising revenues, and to minimise the transaction cost of implementing charges. Likewise, the structure and rate of the charges could be roughly designed as a first step to start the process and send incentive signals to large water users.

To be more cost-effective, charges should be combined with other instruments such as water allocation regimes and minimum ecological river flows (direct regulation) and the promotion of best available technologies (information measures). Charges and their revenues should be an integral part of water resource plans that set priorities and ambition levels for scarcity risk management and guide project financing strategies. Projects should be commensurate with revenue raising capacity and provide visible benefits to water users in the basin; the principle of 'water pays for water' should be introduced so that the river basin agencies can effectively spend the money collected through water charges.

The effect of charges on the affordability of water bills (to which they are passed on) and the competitiveness of water users needs to be documented. Affordability and competitiveness issues should be addressed through targeted accompanying measures rather than exemption or reduction of charges. Reallocation of part of the charge revenues to charge payers would improve acceptability.

The National Water Resources Council (CNRH) created in 1997 at the federal level and State Water Resources Councils (CERHs) should provide clear guidance/criteria on the setting of charge rates and on the use of charge revenues. This should include rate bounds, monitoring and enforcement requirements, assessing side effects such as turning to uncharged water sources, ex ante assessment of costs and benefits of expenditure and publication of accounts. These criteria should aim to set prices according to local risks of scarcity.

Basin states should follow the recommendations of the river basin committee and coordinate on the setting of water charges. To do this, and more generally for better integrated management of the basin's water resources, a single water agency should be created in the interstate basins.

Source: OECD (2017[28]), *Water Charges in Brazil: The Ways Forward*, https://doi.org/10.1787/9789264285712-en.

Box 2.12. Charging for water abstraction and discharges: A checklist

How will the charges scheme link with permitting systems?

- How will your charging scheme fit in with other mechanisms to manage water resources, in particular the use of permits to set limits and conditions on abstraction and discharges? And will your permitting and compliance monitoring systems ensure that charges are calculated fairly and accurately?
- Ideally, the locations of all abstractions and discharges (or nearly all, if a risk-based approach is taken) would be identified and controlled through permits backed by routine compliance monitoring and enforcement where necessary. The permits would then form the basis for the charging scheme and the specific charge related to each user. All abstractions would have a means of measurement designed to ensure compliance with volumetric limits. Other permit conditions, such as restrictions on abstraction at low flows, would also have a means of ensuring

compliance. Discharges should also have a volumetric limit and means of measurement, as well as emission limits to protect the environment and human health for the parameters in the discharge. There should be an agreed basis for monitoring the quality of the discharge at a frequency that meant that the results were statistically significant, auditable and appropriate to the type of process involved.

Designing the charging scheme

- How will you structure the charges so that they align with policy objectives? For both abstractions and discharges, will you use the volume authorised on the permit or the actual volumes abstracted or discharged? The latter requires more effort to oversee: the water user or your inspector will need to record and report the volumes, and there must be a means of measurement of certified accuracy in place (e.g., a calibrated meter) because otherwise, you could be over- or under-charging. Your billing system must also be capable of calculating different charges according to the volume at the billing frequency that you choose.

- Do you want to impose a separate administrative charge to cover the costs of managing and carrying out the technical assessment of applications for new permits or revisions to existing ones?

- Do you want your abstraction charges to send signals about the degree of water stress and incentivise reduced consumption? And what do you mean by "water stress" or "water scarcity"? If it is stress because of excessive abstraction, will you rely on charges alone to achieve a sustainable balance with the available resource or will you also take other measures to reduce abstraction (e.g. by buying out entitlements or by forcible reductions in authorised volumes)? If scarcity is more dynamic, such as from low rainfall and the risk of drought, what will trigger the charging response? And how will you ensure that charge payers are aware of what is happening on a dynamic basis and, where possible, have access to advice about how to reduce their consumption?

- For discharges, what signals do you want to send to polluters and how costly do you want to make the act of pollution? If you want to incentivise a reduction in pollution load from toxic substances, do the permits specify limits on, for example, pesticides, hydrocarbons, metals, cyanides etc.? And how will you reflect this in the charges scheme through a sliding scale from cooling water through to discharges from chemical works and mining operations? If you want to see improved water quality to protect human health and support target ecosystems, can you use charges to help achieve this faster than with progressively tighter limits for environmental-quality-standards-based permits?

- Do you want to send signals about the value of effluent as a resource? In other words, where, when and in what volumes effluent discharges are made is important to other water users (providing that the quality is within permitted limits) and, although these matters can be specified in permits, do you want to reward discharges that benefit resources? Similarly, do you want to penalise abstractions through higher charges where the net return is low because the water has evaporated, been incorporated in a product, lost through leakage or taken up by growing crops?

- How will you ensure that your charging schemes are flexible and adaptable to changes in water demand, environmental stress, climate change and drought? And what feedback mechanism will you build in to allow for periodic reviews of its effectiveness?

Source: OECD (2017[28]), *Water Charges in Brazil: The Ways Forward*, https://doi.org/10.1787/9789264285712-en.

The National Water Law of 1997 introduced charging for water abstractions (cobrança) and provided for the allocation of revenue from charges to water management projects in the basin where they were collected.[1] But feasibility issues (public/political acceptability) have slowed the introduction of abstraction charges in Brazil. Only some states apply them, such as Ceara and Paraiba.

Since 2015, three river basins in the state of Paraíba have introduced abstraction charges (cobrança). However, their implementation is slow, with a recovery rate of less than 10% in 2017 (OECD, 2017[28]). AESA collected USD 890 000 in "cobrança" in 2020. This amount was entirely allocated to projects for the reuse of wastewater in agriculture in the three basins and for the O&M of state reservoirs. In the State of Rio Grande do Norte, drought has made it politically difficult to introduce such abstraction charges (OECD, 2017[28]).

Discussions are underway to introduce abstraction charges in the PPA basin and allocate a portion of the revenues to finance the O&M of the PISF. This could be justified if the public benefits of PISF were demonstrated. In the meantime, the absence of abstraction charges in the PPA basin seriously compromises the financing of the river basin plan (assuming implementation of the water pays for water principle). Indeed, the financial sustainability of CBH is essential in the search for synergies between the allocation of water and integrated water resource management (IWRM) (Figure 2.8).

Figure 2.8. Abstraction charges, water allocation and IWRM: a multifaceted interface

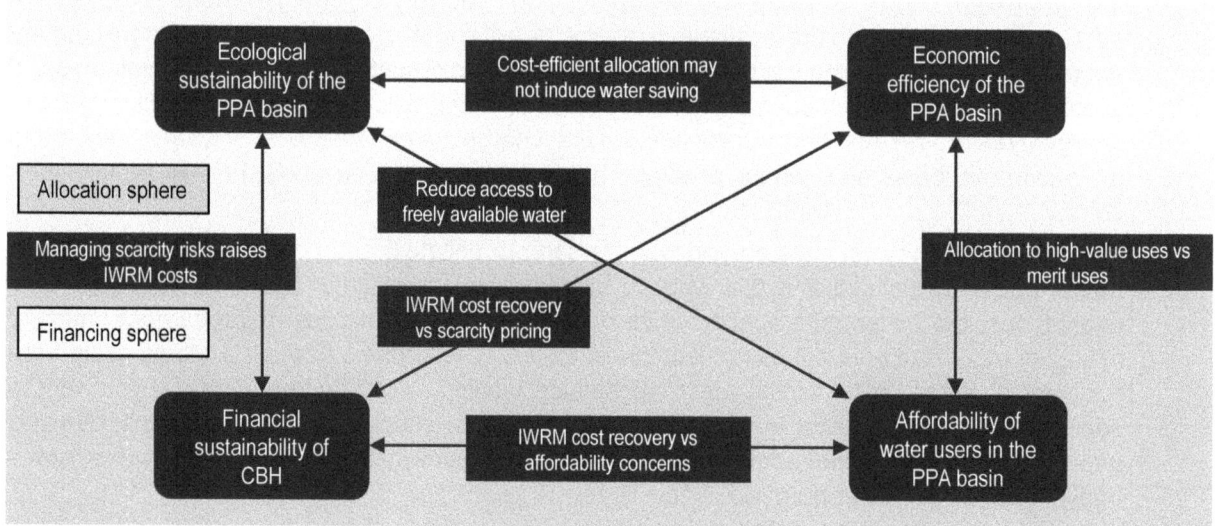

Note: In contrast to pure public goods, "merit goods" are provided through the market, but not necessarily in sufficient quantities to maximise social welfare.
Source: Adapted from Massarutto, A. (2007[29]), "Abstraction charges: How can the theory guide us?", https://www.oecd.org/env/resources/40014641.pdf.

Abstraction charges aim to protect waterbodies from which the water was withdrawn against the risk of scarcity. In France, for example, the Adour-Garonne water agency has different abstraction charge rates depending on the nature and fragility of the water resource withdrawn. Likewise, the allocation of the charge revenues to CBH (in application of the principle of water pays for water) must firstly aim to prevent the risks of water shortage through IWRM.

The charge rate should not vary according to the category of user, as is often the case in OECD countries, where farmers and sometimes industry benefit from preferential rates. As is the case with water tariffs, the water conservation signal would be better preserved by setting the same floor rate for all abstractors, but adding an additional levy on rich abstractors and redistributing income for the poorest to help them pay the floor rate (cross-subsidy between abstractors). Another way to cross-subsidise between rich and poor abstractors without compromising incentives to save water would be to allocate more charge revenues to the poor than they pay out. This is what the Adour Garonne water agency does for the agricultural sector ("principle of solidarity").

Rather than a simple volumetric charge, as put in place by the Adour-Garonne water agency, abstraction charges with an increased block structure could be considered, with a reduced first block size for the water bodies with a high risk of shortage. Any electricity subsidy to abstractors must be removed before introducing an abstraction charge. Box 2.13 provides an overview of the functioning of abstraction charges in France.

> ### Box 2.13. Water abstraction charges in France
>
> Water abstraction charges were introduced in France in 1964, when the six Water Agencies were created. Revenue from charges is collected and redistributed by the Agencies for investments to protect and improve water resources in their respective basins. The charge must be paid by all those who abstract water above a threshold set by each agency (which cannot be more than 10 000 m^3 per year, or 7 000 m^3 in areas with water scarcity). Abstraction at sea, aquaculture-related abstractions, and abstractions outside the low-water period and intended for the restoration of natural areas are exempt.
>
> Water Agencies grant subsidies to water users (farmers, municipalities and industries) funded by abstraction and pollution charges paid by all water users with differentiated rates in each River Basin. For municipalities and domestic users, these charges are collected by water and sanitation services and then transferred to the Water Agency. These charges correspond to a certain extent to resource costs, defined as the opportunity costs of using water as a scarce resource in a particular way (e.g., through abstraction or wastewater discharge) in time and space. Resource costs equal the difference between the economic value in terms of net benefits of present or future water use (e.g., allocation of emission or water abstraction permits) and the economic value in terms of net benefits of the best alternative water use (now or in the future). Resource costs only arise if alternative water use generates a higher economic value than present or foreseen future water use (i.e., the difference between net benefits is negative). Resource costs are therefore not necessarily confined to water resource depletion (in terms of quantity or quality). They arise because of an inefficient allocation (in economic terms) of water and/or pollution over time and across different water users. Normally, environmental and resource costs are partly recovered through environmental taxes and charges (abstraction and pollution charges).
>
> The highest rates are for water used as drinking water. In addition, the rates are differentiated by source (groundwater or surface water) and by zone, to take into account the relative scarcity of water and the pressure that withdrawal exerts on available water resources. As a result, the rate per m^3 of water withdrawn can differ considerably. For example, the rates applied by the Adour-Garonne water agency in 2019-24 range from EUR cent 0.03/m^3 for the filling of canals in an area without water deficit to EUR cent 5.8/m^3 for potable water abstraction in deficit areas (Table 2.3).
>
> The water abstraction charge reflects the "water pays for water" principle and is generally accepted as fair payment for the use of a scarce resource. However, the rates are too low to have a significant impact on water consumption, making the instrument more of a revenue-raising tool than an economic incentive.

Table 2.3. Water abstraction rates in the Adour-Garonne basin

Type of use	Areas with water scarcity			Other areas		
	Rate applied in 2019-24		Ceiling set by law	Rate applied in 2019-24		Ceiling set by law
	Surface water	Groundwater		Surface water	Groundwater	
	EUR cent/m^3			EUR cent/m^3		
Gravity irrigation	1.0	1.0	1.0	0.5	0.5	0.5
Other irrigation	1.22	0.73	7.2	0.92	0.55	3.6
Drinking water	5.8	3.5	14.4	4.4	2.6	7.2
Industrial cooling	0.182	0.109	1.0	0.137	0.082	0.5
Canal filling	0.06	0.06	0.06	0.03	0.03	0.03
Other economic uses	1.57	0.94	10.8	1.18	0.71	5.4

Source: Notice of deliberation of the Board of Directors of the Adour-Garonne water agency of 19 September 2018.

Another issue is the distribution of the burden between users on the basis of a downstream/upstream and urban/rural "solidarity principle", with households paying much more than agriculture and industry. The related rate differentiation contradicts the polluter pays principle. For example, at the Adour-Garonne water agency, 65% of the revenue from abstraction charges is paid by drinking water companies (and passed on to the water bill), much more than their 11% share of the use of water resources (Table 2.4).

Table 2.4. Volume abstracted and charging of abstractions in the Adour-Garonne basin

Water user sector	Water abstraction		Charge revenues	
	Million m^3/year	%	Million EUR/year	%
Households	720	11	40	65
Agriculture	900	14	8	13
Industrial cooling	4 700	71	1	2
Hydropower	-	-	7	11
Other economic uses	320	5	6	10
Total	6 640	100	62	100

Note: - = non-consumptive use.
Source: Adour-Garonne Water Agency (2021[30]), *Homepage*, https://www.eau-grandsudouest.fr/ (accessed December 2021).

In the PPA river basin, there are major water quality problems. In some planning units within the basin, about 85% of sewage is not treated. Municipalities oversee sanitation, but they have limited financial resources to set up proper sanitation. This issue is common to many countries throughout the world, and aggregation of services can be a way forward. In Spain, sanitation is generally done at inter-municipal level thus allowing for a financial solidarity mechanism between large and small municipalities. Small villages that are not able to afford the cost of treatment take part in the planning and water management at inter-municipal level. Some municipalities work with private operators through public-private partnerships for concession or lease contract (for example, in Valencia). In France, water pollution charges are differentiated according to water users, such as households, agriculture and industry – although they can be the same between users. Charges for pollution with domestic origin are based on the water consumption of the household. Table 2.5 compiles the pollution charge for domestic users for the Adour-Garonne River Basin (one of the six river basins in France) and Table 2.6 those for non-domestic users. These charges contrast with those for livestock and pollution with non-domestic origin in agriculture and industry, which are based respectively on number of livestock (above a certain level) and discharged pollutants.

Table 2.5. Pollution charge for domestic users in the Adour-Garonne River Basin, France

Year	2013	2014	2015	2016	2017	2018	Maximum limit set by law
Pollution charge (EUR/m³)	0.3	0.305	0.31	0.315	0.32	0.33	0.5

Table 2.6. Pollution charge for non-domestic users in the Adour-Garonne River Basin, France

Main pollutant elements	Pollution charges (in EUR per unit)						Maximum limit set by law
	2013	2014	2015	2016	2017	2018	
Total dissolved solids (per kg)	0.119	0.122	0.124	0.127	0.129	0.132	0.3
Chemical oxygen demand (COD per kg)	0.074	0.076	0.077	0.079	0.081	0.082	0.2
Biochemical oxygen demand in 5 days (per kg)	0.149	0.152	0.155	0.158	0.161	0.164	0.4
Nitrogen (per kg)	0.3	0.305	0.31	0.315	0.32	0.33	0.7
Nitrates, nitrites (per kg)	0	0	0	0	0	0	0.3
Phosphorus (per kg)	0.4	0.41	0.42	0.43	0.44	0.44	0.2
Metox (per kg)	0.7	0.71	0.73	0.74	0.76	0.77	3.6
Metox for groundwater (per kg)	6	6	6	6	6	6	6
Toxicity high (per kiloequitox)	6.7	6.8	7	7.1	7.2	7.4	18
Toxicity high in groundwater (per kiloequitox)	30	30	30	30	30	30	30
Dangerous substances for the environment in surface water (per kg)				3	4	5	10
Dangerous substances for the environment in groundwater (per kg)				3	4	5	16.6
Dissolved salts (m3 [siemens/centimetre])	0	0	0	0	0	0	0.15
Heated water in sea, except in winter (per megathermie)	1.26	1.29	1.31	1.34	1.37	1.4	8.5
Heated water in river, except in winter (per megathermie)	1.26	1.29	1.31	1.34	1.37	1.4	8.5

Source: OECD (2017[28]), *Water Charges in Brazil: The Ways Forward*, https://doi.org/10.1787/9789264285712-en.

Promoting efficient water use

Tradable permit systems can cost-effectively manage the risk of water scarcity. Water trading refers to the process of buying and selling water rights. The terms of the trade can be either permanent or temporary, depending on the legal status of the water rights. Some economists argue that water trading can promote more efficient water allocation because a market-based price acts as an incentive for users to allocate resources from low-value activities to high-value activities. There are debates about the extent to which water markets operate efficiently in practice, what the social and environmental outcomes of water trading schemes are, and the ethics of applying economic principles to a resource such as water. Water trading markets have been set up in a few countries around the world, including Australia, Chile or the United States. In Arizona and California, these markets are used to re-allocate water rights between farmers and municipalities especially during droughts. These markets provide farmers with revenues while it is cheaper for municipalities to pay farmers not to use water rather than building expensive new water assets.

A bill to introduce water markets was submitted to Congress in 2017, but the text has not been examined yet. In Brazil, rights to use water can be granted to both public and private parties. Water rights do not transfer ownership of water, but allow the use of water for a specific period of time, under specific conditions (OECD, 2017[28]).

Establishing a water market requires setting an abstraction cap that is acceptable to all stakeholders, *including* the environment and local communities. The most cost-effective approach to do this is to build a "risk matrix" that helps manage trade-offs between water uses while protecting the integrity of the water resource. It is also the best way to avoid conflicts of use and to develop a "water culture". The first step is to identify and define (on a scientific basis) the pool of water resources. Second, the risks to water-dependent environmental, cultural and social values ("in situ values") must be assessed as well as the opportunity cost of not taking water for economic development ("development risk"). Third, the acceptable level of water abstraction is set by weighting in situ risks against development risks (the risk matrix). The sophistication of this approach depends on the level of risks incurred (value of the investments envisaged, number of populations dependent on water resources, presence of protected natural areas, etc.).

The geographic scope of a water market should ideally be at the scale of the PPA basin, with the basin being the natural hydrologic unit. However, it is common to organise water markets at the sub-basin (catchment) level, as in Australia, or even at the irrigation district level, as in Chile, for practical (presence of gauges) or administrative feasibility reasons. The greater the number of market participants, the more cost-effective the market is in allocating water. Ideally, all the water in the basin should be involved in the market to preserve the hydrological logic.

The period of validity of water rights should be differentiated according to the risk of water scarcity, as mapped in the PPA basin, with annual allocations for areas at risk and longer-term entitlements for areas well provided with water. The latter would obtain higher quotations on the markets because they offer greater security of supply.

Part of the proceeds from the auction of water rights would cover the operating costs of the market (brokers, etc.) but the majority would be allocated to financing IWRM. Public funds for the rural development policy could partially offset the impact on local communities of permanent transfers of water rights to another region. However, if unregulated permanent transfers would be allowed, there is a risk of concentrating water in the hands of a few wealthy water users, who could buy off all the water from numerous small water users. This can have consequences on the local and regional social dynamics, unemployment rates and demographic migrations. Therefore, a proper framework to access the costs and benefits of water market is recommended, as proposed by Wheeler et al. and Grafton (2017[31]; 2019[32]). According to that framework, the existing governance and institutional arrangements and the costs and benefits from trade should be evaluated before the water market implementation. Then, institutional and policy changes should be implemented, including water rights registration and monitoring and enforcement capabilities. Finally, externalities should be continuously monitored and market changes should be implemented as required.

Arrangements should be made to prevent hoarding – such as through 'use it or lose it' policy – and regulatory capture by the market operator. Satellite monitoring combined with modelling of stream flow could help monitor and enforce water rights to surface waters. Boxes Box 2.14 and 2.15 provide an overview of the functioning of water markets in the western United States and in the Murray-Darling Basin, Australia.

Box 2.14. Water markets in the western United States

Property right to water

Since 1850, California applies riparian rights for water. The right entitles a landowner to use water on land that he owns adjacent to a stream ("riparian" land). The landowner is allowed to make "reasonable use" of the water if this does not impact the rights of other riparian owners. However, no specific quantity attaches to a riparian right, which is de facto subject to imprecise sharing in the event of a shortage.

This arrangement may work in a region with abundant surface water but not in an arid region, which is why California introduced appropriative water rights in 1855 (while retaining riparian rights). Colorado introduced prior appropriation in 1876 and repealed its riparian doctrine in 1882. Appropriative rights differ fundamentally from riparian rights. They are based on the time and the quantity of the initial diversion (first in time, first in right). In case of water shortage, priority ranking is based on seniority.

However, the transfer of an appropriative right is not a simple transaction between two parties. All the western states of the United States have a legacy of unreliable records due to the slapdash way many appropriative rights were created in the 19th Century. This is an impediment to transferring water rights to another party. Another is the no-injury rule. The rule stipulates that changes in a water right shall not adversely impact the water right of any third party, whether junior or senior. If harm is claimed, the onus is on the transferor, not the challenger, to prove no third-party injury. In Colorado, for example, any impact from a transfer, no matter how small or far in the future, constitutes an injury.

Besides these two impediments to the transferability of appropriative water rights, most western states declare in their constitution that their waters belong to the people of the state. It does give the state an interest in how the water is used and transferred for the public benefit. The distinctive public interest in the use of water also means that all water use must be "reasonable". This renders all water rights fragile. A water right that was reasonable when first recognised may become unreasonable as hydrologic conditions change. For example, in 1983, the California Supreme Court made the landmark ruling that a 1940 appropriation right could be modified ex post because of harm now occurring to Mono Lake.

When do water markets occur?

Physical connectivity between seller and buyer is crucial for exchanging water. For example, in California's southern San Joaquin Valley, the construction in 1975 of a canal connecting the aqueducts of the federal Central Valley Project (CVP) to the east and the State Water Project (SWP) to the west generated a cascade of water exchanges. Another example is the trans-mountain tunnel that conveys Colorado River water from western to eastern Colorado. By special legal treatment, the no-injury rule does not apply to the transferred waters, which are no longer subject to prior appropriation once transferred to the east (more precisely the Colorado-Big Thompson project, C-BT). C-BT contracts make all units of water equal and transferable. While data is incomplete, it appears that most of the surface water transferred in the US West was "contract water" moving within supply system boundaries, for example, in the C-BT system in Colorado and the SWP/CVP systems in California.

It is widely held that there needs to be significant re-allocation of water use in the US West. However, over the period 1990-2010, most surface water transferred involved one-year leases, providing short-term flexibility, not long-term re-allocation (only about 5-10% of the amount transferred annually was transferred long-term or permanently). Modification of the property right to water is essential if there is to be more significant long-run reallocation of water use given the complexities in existing water rights.

Source: Hanemann, M. and M. Young (2020[33]), "Water rights reform and water marketing: Australia vs the US West", https://doi.org/10.1093/oxrep/grz037.

> **Box 2.15. Water markets in the Murray–Darling Basin, Australia**
>
> The Murray-Darling Basin (MDB) covers 14% of mainland Australia. The volume of water demand from cities and for energy production is minor compared with the requirements for environmental flows and irrigation. Three quarters of Australia's irrigated crops and pastures are grown in the Basin.
>
> The MDB is characterised by an extreme variability of river inflows. The risks of irrigation water shortage resulting from over-allocation of irrigation water led authorities to close the allocation of new water entitlements. In addition, a cap on water use was introduced in 1995 to limit extraction of water from the MDB to 1993-94 levels. This was the first step to introducing water trading into the MDB. Unbundling water entitlements from the right to use and own land was instrumental in the development of a functioning water market in the MDB, which took more than a decade between 1994 and 2006. Unbundling allows water to be transferred independently of land between users, without the need to consider land use requirements.
>
> The establishment of water markets also provides a mechanism to address the risks of environmental water shortage through reallocating water between irrigators and the environment. In 2002, a first step was taken in reallocating water to the environment, through the Living Murray Initiative. The Water Act (2007) went further by providing for a sustainable diversion limit (SDL) for each river and groundwater management area in the MDB, for implementation in 2019.
>
> The Basin Plan (2012) sets the amount of environmental water that needs to be recovered to meet SDLs. In 2008 nearly AUD 9 (USD 7.5) billion had been provided to recover water for the environment through increased irrigation efficiency such as on-farm irrigation upgrades, upgraded water delivery infrastructure and metering (65%), and buybacks of water entitlements (35%). In 2012, the federal government committed a further AUD 1.8 (USD 1.8) billion to address operational constraints restricting the regulated delivery of environmental water throughout the MDB. Around 4 000 GL/year should be recovered by 2025, 55% via water buybacks and 45% via savings and infrastructure, compared to the long-term average water use in irrigation of 11 000 GL/year.
>
> In this way, the management of environmental flows in the MDB shifted from direct regulation to a combination of direct regulation and tradable permit system (buybacks of water entitlements), introducing more flexibility. On the other hand, subsidising irrigation infrastructure to increase environmental flows is not cost-effective; the average cost per litre of environmental water has been estimated up to six times that of direct purchases of water entitlements.
>
> There are two types of water entitlements in the MDB depending on their level of security. The availability of water for holders of "general security" entitlements is announced as a proportion of entitlement, commonly referred to as an "allocation". The announced allocation depends on the resources currently available in storage and the resources expected to be available during the season. "High security" water entitlements generally have their allocated water delivered each year even though they are also subject to announced allocations. Allowing for two types of water entitlements with varying levels of security allow users to express different risk preferences reflected in the price of entitlements.
>
> Source: Grafton, Q. and J. Horne (2014[34]), "Water markets in the Murray-Darling Basin", http://dx.doi.org/10.22459/GW.05.2014.08.

Combining policy instruments

Instrument combinations may increase cost-effectiveness and public acceptability against the use of an economic instrument alone in meeting PPA basin management objectives. Here, we look at three combinations of instruments: (1) abstraction charges and water markets; (2) abstraction charges and direct regulation; and (3) water markets and direct regulation.

Abstraction charges and water markets

Applied to the same target group, the effect of introducing abstraction charges in the presence of a water market (cap-and-trade of water permits) differs according to the rate of the charges. Charges set at a rate lower than the initial market price do not change the overall level of abstraction set by the cap but reduce the demand for water permits; the market price will gradually align with the charge rate (if all abstractors are obligated under both instruments). If the charge rate is higher than the market price, the incentive for marginal abatement (water saving) is increased, the abatement then exceeding the cap set by the water market. The demand for water permits, and therefore their price, would then drop to zero, with abstraction charges being the only active instrument.

Despite such apparent incompatibility in terms of effectiveness, the combination of instruments could improve cost-efficiency when abstraction charges are used to secure a minimum market price ("floor price"), again if all abstractors are obligated under both instruments (i.e., if the two instruments apply to the same abstraction units). While a floor price can reduce static efficiency in situations where the water market would otherwise produce permit prices below the floor value, such an effect, as well as the relative price certainty it engenders, usually increases dynamic cost-efficiency compared to a "pure" tradable permit system (TPS). The use of a floor price would also help capture windfall rents created by free permit allocation. Abstraction charges could also be used to secure a "ceiling price" (or "safety valve price") by allowing abstractors to withdraw water for which they do not hold a permit in return for an abstraction charge at a ceiling rate. However, if a ceiling price provides TPS participants with certainty about the costs of compliance, it reduces certainty about the environmental outcome and can reduce dynamic incentives.

Abstraction charges and water markets can lead to creating water scarcity geographically, sectorally and temporally (i.e., creating a "hot spot" of scarcity). Applying an additional charge to participants in a water market located in a sub-basin where withdrawal creates higher marginal scarcity than in other sub-basins can resolve this problem. Figure 2.9 illustrates this concept. Abstractor B, whose abstraction produces much higher marginal damage to water scarcity than other abstractors, is subject to both the water market and the abstraction charge, which increases its incentive to save water. If the charge rate is equal to the differential between the permit price and the total marginal damages on water scarcity of the abstraction concerned, as illustrated, then total static cost-efficiency is maintained and the overall efficiency is increased (although the prices of the permits decrease if the water market cap is not adjusted to compensate).

Although the combination of price and quantity-based instruments may produce greater welfare than either one alone, very few of these combinations have been used in practice. Applying an abstraction charge alongside a water market increases the administrative burden on participants and relevant authorities. The transaction costs associated with implementing and administering a water market increase with the use of price floors and ceilings. However, hybrid price-quantity instruments improve flexibility to deal with uncertainties. A floor price in a cap-and-trade system provides a continued incentive to save water if the marginal costs of saving water are overestimated (as well as minimal revenue generation), while a price ceiling prevents excessive costs if the marginal costs of saving water are underestimated (along with maximum compliance cost certainty). Likewise, a cap provides the certainty of water saving that an abstraction charge alone cannot provide (thus reducing the aversion to the charge).

Figure 2.9. Combining an abstraction charge with a tradable permit system to address water scarcity hot spots

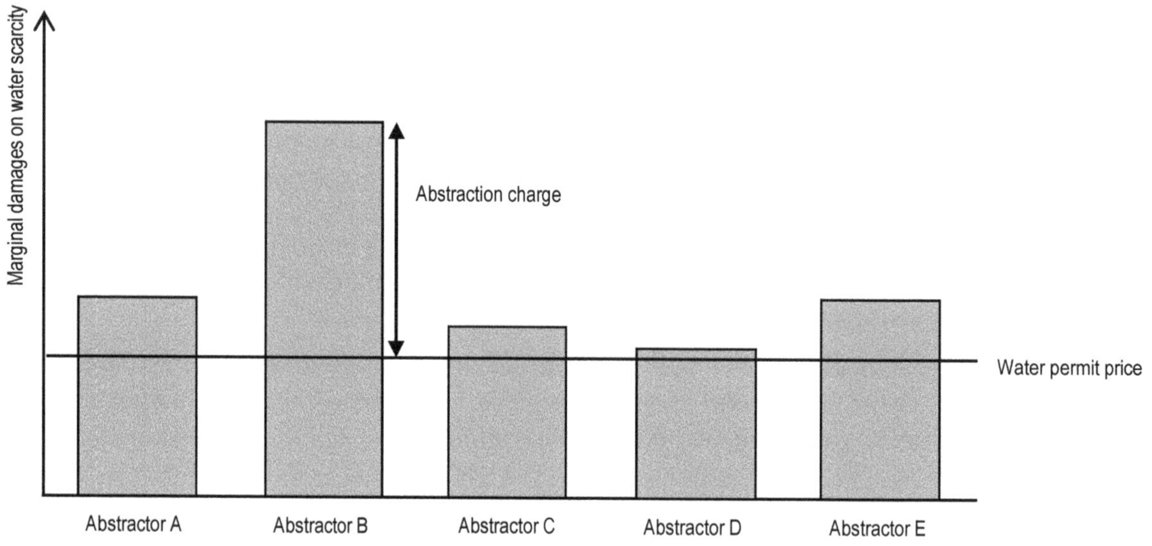

Source: Adapted from Drummond, M. et al. (2015[35]), *Methods for the Economic Evaluation of Health Care Programmes, 4th ed.*, Oxford University Press.

Abstraction charges and direct regulation

When both instruments target the same abstractors, direct regulation helps overcome market failures (e.g. principal-agent problems) and information failures that hamper the effectiveness of pricing instruments. Conversely, abstraction charges can reduce the "rebound" effect that direct regulation can induce.[2] Direct regulation combined with a pricing instrument can also reduce the occurrence of water scarcity hot spots; while pricing instruments influence total water withdrawal, direct regulation can influence the location of abstraction and its timing.

In terms of cost-efficiency, the addition of direct regulation to an abstraction charge would seem superfluous if the marginal cost of water savings implied by the regulation is lower than the value of the charge. Indeed, abstractors would have already complied with such regulation to achieve water savings at a cost lower than the charge. Figure 2.10 illustrates this for a given abstractor for which water savings are required or incentivised by regulation. But in the real world, static efficiency is increased if the regulation requires or induces water savings with marginal costs less than the value of the abstraction charge (e.g., stringency level A to level C in Figure 2.10) that would not have been achieved due to market failures. However, if the water savings levels required by regulation have a higher marginal cost than the value of the abstraction charge, then the charge will not result in any additional water saving (e.g., stringency levels D and E in Figure 2.10).

Generally, for a given level of water savings, combining a pricing instrument with direct regulation would often be more cost-efficient than using direct regulation alone, as the pricing instruments equalise the marginal incentive of water savings where direct regulation cannot. In addition, a predictable (pre-planned) increase in the stringency of regulatory requirements and abstraction charge rates increases dynamic cost-efficiency.

Figure 2.10. Cost-efficiency of a combination of abstraction charge and direct regulation

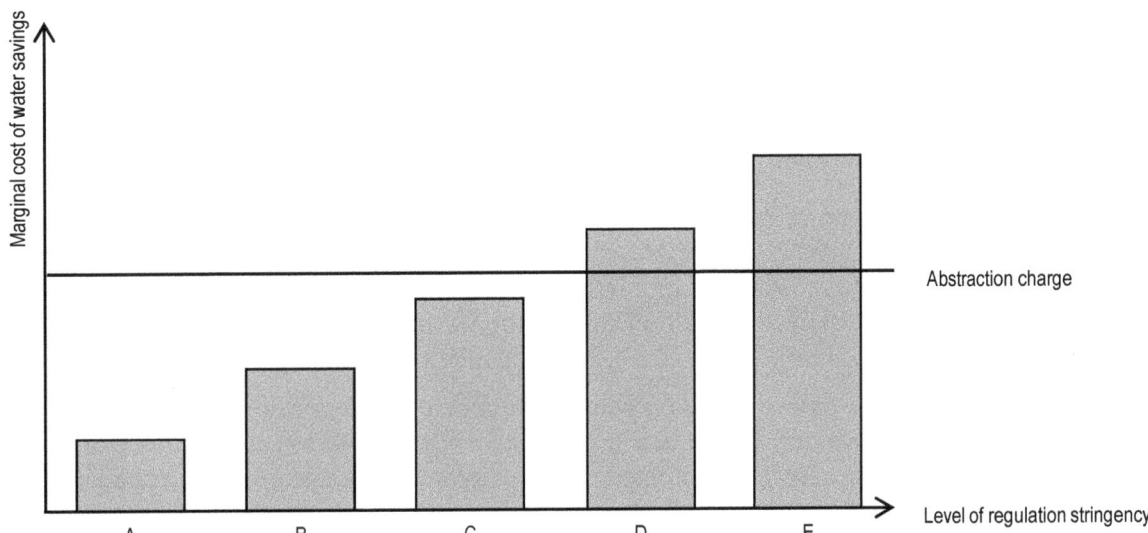

Source: Adapted from Drummond, M. et al. (2015[35]), *Methods for the Economic Evaluation of Health Care Programmes*, 4th ed., Oxford University Press.

By combining a pricing instrument and direct regulation to tackle the occurrence of scarcity hot spots, static cost-efficiency is maintained, with potential overall efficiency increased if the additional marginal cost of water savings from the secondary instrument is equal to the difference between the marginal cost of the primary instrument and the marginal damage to water scarcity.[3] As discussed above, this is also the case with the combination of an abstraction charge and a TPS (Figure 2.9).

A well-designed combination of direct regulation and abstraction charges would be more publicly and politically acceptable than resorting to a high charge rate or stringent regulation to achieve a given level of water savings. Using regulation to supplement an abstraction charge can reduce uncertainty about short-term and longer-term actions to save water, especially if the charge rate is set too low (compared to water saving costs).[4] However, the flexibility of this combination is likely to decrease as the stringency of regulation increases.

Water markets and direct regulation

Direct regulation can be used to supplement a water market to prevent water scarcity hot spots. However, supplementing a water market with direct regulation of any design, scope and level of stringency will not reduce the total volume of water abstracted, which, *ceteris paribus*, will remain on aggregate at the level of the cap. Likewise, the use of water markets to support direct regulation does not reduce the aggregate water savings beyond what would be expected from the use of regulation alone (because once each abstractor meets its regulatory requirements, the demand for and the price of water permits drops to zero).

A water market (an aggregate limit imposed by a cap-and-trade system) can be used to increase flexibility and reduce the cost of complying with regulation specific to subgroups (e.g. sector, irrigation district, type of industry). Abstractors that outperform regulation can generate credits that the underperformers can buy to fill their deficit. This is the essence of a baseline-and-credit system.

Using direct regulation to supplement a water market has a positive impact on static and dynamic cost-efficiency if regulation reduces market and information failures that limit the influence of the price signal produced by the water market. However, the regulation must require or incentivise the use of technologies or behaviours with a marginal cost of water savings below that of the permit price to maintain static cost-efficiency. Otherwise, total compliance costs are increased with permit demand and prices likely reducing in response, diminishing the efficiency benefits of a water market.

An exception to this is when a direct regulation attempts to address water scarcity hotspots, with marginal costs of water savings imposed that are equal to the difference between the permit price and the total marginal damages on water scarcity of the abstraction concerned. In such cases, static cost-efficiency is maintained, and overall economic efficiency is increased.

Using a water market in addition to regulation can achieve a given level of water savings more cost-efficiently (both statically and dynamically) than using direct regulation alone. This is because pricing instruments equalise the marginal incentive to save water when direct regulation cannot. However, to maintain cost-efficiency the cap or baseline of the TPS must be set considering the water savings expected from the regulation.

Political acceptability is likely to differ depending on which instrument is primary and which is secondary. Using direct regulation to resolve hot spot issues in a water market is likely to increase the total costs of compliance, thereby reducing acceptability compared to a single water market. The same applies to more general regulations (e.g. broadly applicable minimum performance or technology standards), even if the measures or behaviours induced have marginal costs lower than that of the permit price, the reduction in flexibility that this represents may reduce acceptability. Additionally, the nature of a water market means that permit prices are likely to vary over time - perhaps substantially. While it can lead to inefficiencies and reduced feasibility, a supplementary direct regulation can help address uncertainties and ensure a minimum level of environmental effectiveness in the short (and potentially long) term. On the other hand, by adding a water market to a regulatory instrument, increasing flexibility and the possibility of reducing compliance costs, acceptability and the ability to deal with uncertainties can be increased.

References

Adour-Garonne Water Agency (2021), *Homepage*, https://www.eau-grandsudouest.fr/ (accessed on 10 December 2021). [30]

ANA (2016), *Background report on setting and governing economic instruments for water policy in Brazil*. [7]

ANA (2016), "Plano de recursos hídricos da bacia hidrográfica do rio Piancó-Piranhas-Açu - Resumo executivo", Agência Nacional de Águas, http://piranhasacu.ana.gov.br/produtos/PRH_PiancoPiranhasAcu_ResumoExecutivo_30062016.pdf. [2]

ANA (2014), *Cobrança pelo Uso de Recursos Hídricos, Cadernos de capacitação em recursos hídricos, Vol. 7.*, https://arquivos.ana.gov.br/institucional/sge/CEDOC/Catalogo/2014/CadernosdeCapacitacaoemRecursosHidricosVol7.pdf (accessed on 4 January 2022). [5]

CBH PPA (n.d.), *Relatorio*, http://cbhpiancopiranhasacu.org.br/docs/relatorio/tdrplanopiranhasacu_final-1.pdf. [6]

City of Cape Town (2019), *Cape Town Water Strategy*, https://resource.capetown.gov.za/documentcentre/Documents/City%20strategies%2c%20plans%20and%20frameworks/Cape%20Town%20Water%20Strategy.pdf. [16]

Cox, A. and P. Börkey (2015), "Challenges and policy options for financing urban water and sanitation" January, pp. 68-92, http://dx.doi.org/10.4324/9781315848440-14. [27]

da Silva Santos, A. (2021), "Ex-post evaluation of the socio-economic consequences of the Integration Project of the São Francisco River with Watersheds of the Northern Northeast", *CADERNOS DE FINANÇAS PÚBLICAS*, Vol. 21/1, https://publicacoes.tesouro.gov.br/index.php/cadernos/article/view/128 (accessed on 4 January 2022). [8]

de Lucena Barbosa, J. et al. (2021), "Impacts of inter-basin water transfer on the water quality of receiving reservoirs in a tropical semi-arid region", *Hydrobiologia*, Vol. 848/3, pp. 651-673, http://dx.doi.org/10.1007/S10750-020-04471-Z/FIGURES/8. [9]

de Sousa Freitas, M. (2021), "The Piancó-Piranhas-Açu Hydrographic Basin Face to the 2012-2020 Drought Event", *Brazilian Journal of Animal and Environmental Research*, Vol. 4/1, pp. 1033-1046, http://dx.doi.org/10.34188/bjaerv4n1-084. [3]

Drummond, M. et al. (2015), *Methods for the Economic Evaluation of Health Care Programmes. 4th ed.*, Oxford University Press. [35]

Glauber, J. et al. (2021), "Design principles for agricultural risk management policies", *OECD Food, Agriculture and Fisheries Papers*, No. 157, OECD Publishing, Paris, https://dx.doi.org/10.1787/1048819f-en. [22]

Grafton, Q. and J. Horne (2014), "Water markets in the Murray-Darling Basin", http://dx.doi.org/10.22459/GW.05.2014.08. [34]

Grafton, R. (2019), "Policy review of water reform in the Murray-Darling Basin, Australia: the "do's" and "do'nots"", *Australian Journal of Agricultural and Resource Economics*, Vol. 63/1, pp. 116-141, http://dx.doi.org/10.1111/1467-8489.12288. [32]

Hanemann, M. and M. Young (2020), "Water rights reform and water marketing: Australia vs the US West", *Oxford Review of Economic Policy*, Vol. 36/1, pp. 108-131, https://doi.org/10.1093/oxrep/grz037. [33]

IBGE (2011), *Atlas de saneamento : 2011 / IBGE, Diretoria de Geociências*, https://biblioteca.ibge.gov.br/biblioteca-catalogo?id=253096&view=detalhes (accessed on 5 January 2022). [1]

IBGE (2006), *Censo Agropecuário 2006*. [4]

Inter-American Development Bank (2016), *The Potential of Land Value Capture for Financing Urban Projects: Methodological Considerations and Case Studies*, https://publications.iadb.org/publications/english/document/The-Potential-of-Land-Value-Capture-for-Financing-Urban-Projects-Methodological-Considerations-and-Case-Studies.pdf (accessed on 7 January 2022). [26]

Kibel, P. (2014), "WTO Recourse for Reclamation Irrigation Subsidies: Undermarket Water Prices as Foregone Revenue", *Publications*, https://digitalcommons.law.ggu.edu/pubs/647 (accessed on 4 January 2022). [24]

Martuwarra Fitzroy River (2016), *Fitzroy River Declaration*, https://martuwarrafitzroyriver.org/fitzroy-river-declaration. [17]

Massarutto, A. (2007), "Abstraction charges: How can the theory guide us?", OECD, Paris, https://www.oecd.org/env/resources/40014641.pdf. [29]

Mathijssen, D. et al. (2020), "Potential impact of floating solar panels on water quality in reservoirs; pathogens and leaching", *Water Practice and Technology*, Vol. 15/3, pp. 807-811, http://dx.doi.org/10.2166/WPT.2020.062. [25]

Ministério da Integração Nacional (2004), *Relatório de Impacto Ambiental da Transposição*. [10]

OECD (2021), *Water Governance in Cape Town, South Africa*, OECD Studies on Water, OECD Publishing, Paris, https://doi.org/10.1787/a804bd7b-en. [15]

OECD (2018), *Implementing the OECD Principles on Water Governance: Indicator Framework and Evolving Practices*, OECD Studies on Water, OECD Publishing, Paris, https://doi.org/10.1787/9789264292659-en. [13]

OECD (2017), *Water Charges in Brazil: The Ways Forward*, OECD Studies on Water, OECD Publishing, Paris, https://dx.doi.org/10.1787/9789264285712-en. [28]

OECD (2015), *Stakeholder Engagement for Inclusive Water Governance*, OECD Studies on Water, OECD Publishing, Paris, https://dx.doi.org/10.1787/9789264231122-en. [14]

OECD (2015), *Water Resources Allocation: Sharing Risks and Opportunities*, OECD Studies on Water, OECD Publishing, Paris, https://dx.doi.org/10.1787/9789264229631-en. [20]

OECD (2015), *Water Resources Governance in Brazil*, OECD Studies on Water, OECD Publishing, Paris, https://dx.doi.org/10.1787/9789264238121-en. [19]

OECD (2011), *Water Governance in OECD Countries: A Multi-level Approach*, OECD Studies on Water, OECD Publishing, Paris, https://dx.doi.org/10.1787/9789264119284-en. [12]

OECD/ANA (2021), "Workshop on Strengthening River Basin Governance in the Piancó-Piranhas Açu River Basin (25-28 May 2021)". [18]

OECD/ANA (2019-21), "Water Governance Workshops". [11]

Poff, L., R. Tharme and A. Arthington (2017), "Evolution of environmental flows assessment science, principles, and methodologies", http://dx.doi.org/10.1016/B978-0-12-803907-6.00011-5. [21]

UNESCO (2021), "Irrigators' tribunals of the Spanish Mediterranean coast: The Council of Wise Men of the plain of Murcia and the Water Tribunal of the plain of Valencia", United Nations Educational, Scientific and Cultural Organization, https://ich.unesco.org/en/RL/irrigators-tribunals-of-the-spanish-mediterranean-coast-the-council-of-wise-men-of-the-plain-of-murcia-and-the-water-tribunal-of-the-plain-of-valencia-00171. [23]

Wheeler, S. et al. (2017), "Developing a water market readiness assessment framework", *Journal of Hydrology*, Vol. 552, pp. 807-820, http://dx.doi.org/10.1016/j.jhydrol.2017.07.010. [31]

Annex 2.A. Action plan

The tables summarise the main actions presented in Chapter 2.

Annex Table 2.A.1. Strengthening multi-level governance and the use of economic instruments in the Piancó-Piranhas Açu River Basin

Adopt a governance arrangement that ensures water management at the appropriate scale and foster effective coordination	Make use of existing State Agencies and check that all roles and responsibilities are clearly defined and allocated among them; to this end, conduct a self-assessment to assess the state of play of water governance policy frameworks (what), institutions (who) and instruments (how), and their needed improvements over time, for all water functions (water resources management, water services provisioning and water disaster risk reduction).
	Following the principle of subsidiarity, find and agree with all relevant stakeholders on the smallest appropriate scale to fulfil the water management functions as identified in the previous step.
	Evaluate whether catchment-based institutions are delivering their mandates (once they have been clearly defined and allocated) using performance to identify gaps and plan measures to overcome them.
Strengthen stakeholder engagement	Produce and share comprehensive information and material to all stakeholders to build trust, to fuel discussion on common grounds while fostering transparency and common understanding of the situation at catchment level.
	Pay specific attention to the involvement of municipalities in water resources management using tailored communication methods and tools, with interactive and remote meetings as well as in-person meetings in different municipalities.
	Make a tailored effort to reach out to underserved/disadvantaged communities considering traditional and environmental values, valuing historical and ecological knowledge of native communities.
Invest in monitoring and hydrology control	Make it mandatory for a water right holder to install a control system and report information on water withdrawal, with possible removal of water rights in case of repeated non-reporting or inaccurate reporting; increase enforcement capacity with a mix of control mechanisms (people on the ground, tele-detection, etc.).
	Require more detailed assessments of water availability and use are in areas of water stress; make more stringent rules for water resources management and allocation in these areas with greater enforcement capacity.
	Use hydrology models as a tool to foster dialogue among water stakeholders, and support informed decision-making; share hydrology model information with stakeholders to provide a better understanding of the hydrological situation and its likely evolution.
Finance the operation and maintain bulk water infratsructure	Require users (e.g. state water agencies) to fully cover the costs of operating and maintaining federal reservoirs; to this end, work towards the approval of the bill recently submitted to Congress by the Ministry of Regional Development.
	Require that the four states served by the São Francisco River Integration Project (PISF), namely Ceará, Paraíba, Pernambuco and Rio Grande do Norte, fully cover the operating and maintenance costs of the PISF; to this end, work towards the revision of user charges ("*serviço de adução de água bruta*") provided for by the ANA.
	As a transitional step towards recovery of O&M costs through user charges ("*serviço de adução de água bruta*"), consider mobilising other sources of funding, such as, allocating part of the revenue from abstraction charges ("*cobrança*"), provided that the public benefits of bulk water supply are demonstrated (e.g., regulation of river flow); earmarking the increase in land tax revenues linked to the increase in the price of land served by bulk water infrastructure (value capture); and, payment for ecosystem services for bulk water infrastructure using nature-based solutions.
Water allocation and abstraction charges	Extend the coverage of abstraction charges ("*cobrança*") to the entire Piancó-Piranhas-Açu river basin, as provided for in the 1997 National Water Law; differentiate the charge rates according to the risk of water shortage (and not according to users) to protect waterbodies from which the water was withdrawn against the risk of scarcity.
	Allocate revenue from abstraction charges ("*cobrança*") to water resources management projects in the basin where they were collected, applying the principle of water pays for water with the aim to prevent the risks of water shortage.
Water allocation and water market	For water bodies with chronic water deficit, set limits on the total volume of water available for allocation (i.e., an abstraction cap) that is acceptable to all stakeholders, including environment and communities; to this end, include a risk matrix in each water resource compact ("*marco regulatório*).
	Differentiate the term of validity of water rights according to the risk of water scarcity, with annual allocations for areas at risk and longer-term entitlements for areas well provided with water.
	Consider auctioning water rights throughout the Piancó-Piranhas-Açu river basin and allocating the proceeds of the auction to finance water scarcity risk management projects in the basin.
	Consider combining abstraction charges ("*cobrança*") and water markets to guarantee a minimum market price ("floor price") and avoid water scarcity "hot spots" by applying the charge where trade creates a shortage.
	Continue to cover the risk of non-production instead of seeking to cover the risk of lack of irrigation water; design

Agricultural insurance to compensate farmers for unserved irrigation water rights	agricultural risk management instruments that support income decoupled from agricultural production.
	Define an "acceptable level" of drought risk as a threshold when setting insurance premiums; it will also help to address adverse selection problems.
	Instead of subsidising the insurance premium for poor farmers, apply a floor premium to all farmers, introduce an additional premium for the rich and redistribute income to the poorest to help them pay the floor premium; it will also help to address moral hazard issues.

Notes

[1] Homogeneity of geomorphological, hydrographic and hydrological factors characterises the Hydrological Planning Units (UPH). UPHs include subdivisions of the river basin, sub-basins of tributary rivers, or segments of main rivers with spatial continuity.

[1] Article 22 of the water law caps administrative costs at 7.5% of the total collected.

[2] The rebound effect occurs when increasing water use efficiency reduces the cost per unit of agricultural or industrial goods produced (or per unit of water supplied to end users), increasing water consumption according to the price elasticity of demand for those goods or services.

[3] A 'primary' instrument provides the general incentive or requirement for water savings, with a broader scope than the 'secondary' instrument with which it is combined.

[4] A regulation requiring the adoption of a given technology (e.g. drip irrigation) often induces a more permanent change than the water-saving incentives that a pricing instrument can induce, which can be reversed after the price signal is reduced or removed.

3 Making water and sanitation regulation in Brazil more effective

Infrastructure development should be accompanied by effective regulatory oversight and monitoring. The 2020 Sanitation Law of Brazil brought changes to ANA's regulatory and operational role while raising several challenges, from how it can adapt its mandate and develop its capacity and resources, to how it can embrace issuing standards for service and sanitation, oversight of sub-national authorities and promoting the regionalisation of service provision. This chapter summarises the implications and challenges of the new Sanitation Law and provides examples from international practices as well as relevant OECD normative guidance.

The 2020 sanitation law

The new Sanitation Law (Law 14.206 of 15 July 2020) marks the reform of the regulatory framework for water and sanitation in Brazil. In addition to expanding ANA's role from water resource management to defining reference standards for water sanitation services (WSS) and overseeing their application by sub-national authorities (Figure 3.1), the new framework provides increased opportunities for privatisation and private investment, with the aim of developing infrastructure and expanding sanitation services throughout the country (universal provision). This is an important change for the sector, as under the previous legal framework, WSS was regulated locally without federal direction or supervision, which led to dispersed, un-harmonised and unbalanced rules, creating inefficiencies and regulatory risks. The new Sanitation Law is expected to create a more stable regulatory environment.

Figure 3.1. Evolution of the role of ANA

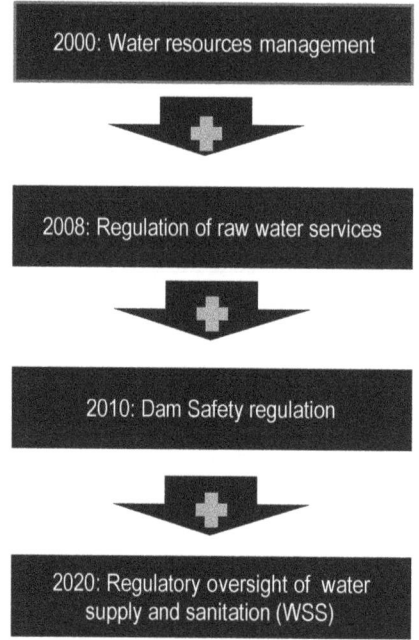

Sources: Official Journal of the Union (2020[1]), *Law 14.026 of 15 July 2020*, https://www.in.gov.br/en/web/dou/-/lei-n-14.026-de-15-de-julho-de-2020-267035421; ANA (2021[2]), *Homepage*, https://www.ana.gov.br/eng/ (accessed on 20 November 2021); SNIS (2018[3]), *The National Sanitation Information System*, http://www.snis.gov.br/painel-informacoes-saneamento-brasil/web/painel-setor-saneamento.

The main outcome sought by the new national sanitation framework is the universalisation of provision, with the goal of supplying 99% of the population with drinking water and providing sewage collection and treatment to 90% of the population by the end of 2033.[1] A number of means are outlined in the new Sanitation Law for the achievement of the main goal, chiefly the harmonisation of approaches and standards at sub-national authorities through the adoption of ANA-issued reference standards, capacity building at sub-national authorities, regionalisation and the enhancement of private sector access.

ANA was placed at the centre of the reform, becoming the national regulator for the WSS sector. In particular, ANA has been tasked with the formulation of reference standards, to be followed on a formal voluntary basis by the sub-national authorities, and with the responsibility to guide local regulatory agencies and service providers (in the form of preparing technical studies, guides and manuals, as well as promoting human resource training) (Figure 3.1 and Table 3.1).

Table 3.1. Main changes to ANA roles and responsibilities in the 2020 Sanitation Law

Before the 2020 Sanitation Law	Additional responsibilities of ANA in the 2020 Sanitation Law
National Policy for Water Resources • Water resources plans • Classification of water bodies according to use • Granting of rights for the use of water resources • Charging for the use of water • System of Information on Water Resources National System of Water Resources Management (SINGREH) • Management support, monitoring and planning of water resources • Information for improvement of the performance of water resources management agencies and of the sectors that use these resources • Encouragement of the creation of river basin committees, particularly in rivers under Federal Government domain • Programmes and projects promoting the spread of practices related to the use of the water resources, and the ecological health of water basins • Dissemination of periodic information on the condition of Brazilian water basins	Establishment and monitoring of **reference standards** for sub-national authorities to: • Stimulate co-operation between federal entities with a focus on universal standardisation of contractual instruments and tariff regulation • promote the regionalisation of service provision • improve the standards of quality and efficiency in the provision, maintenance and operation of services • establish criteria to limit duplication of administrative or managerial costs to be paid by the end user **Oversight** of compliance with those standards • through periodic verification by ANA on the adoption of reference standards • reporting on verification results for the purposes of sub-national authorities' access to federal funding **Capacity-building of sub-national authorities**: responsibility to guide and educate service providers, local regulatory agencies and service providers, as well as to prepare technical studies, guides and manuals, and promote human resource training Voluntary **mediation or arbitration** in disputes involving granting authorities, regulatory agencies or public basic sanitation service providers Encourage forming **blocks of local government authorities** to provide services to third parties, allowing less viable locations to combine, enabling private investment (**regionalisation**)
Main stakeholders: • National Council of Water Resources (CNRH) • State councils of water resources • Watershed committees • Federal, state and municipal institutions responsible for water resources management and water agencies	Main stakeholders: • Federal, state and municipal institutions responsible for WSS and sub-national regulators • Federal government • Providers of private finance • Consumer groups
WSS regulation responsibility: municipal and state level with no federal involvement	WSS regulation responsibility: municipal and state level with federal-level oversight from ANA

The successful delivery of the new legal framework has the potential to raise challenges for the various actors involved. First, Brazil is a vast continental country, with many realities: social inequality, geographical and cultural differences across its regions, and low capacity to pay for services, all of which are intensified by the COVID-19 crisis, as well as uneven capacity of state-level actors. A process of harmonising regulations with the aim of achieving universal access to WSS for Brazilian citizens in this context will require engagement and flexibility from all actors involved. According to SNIS (National System of Information for Sanitation) data, in 2018 only 83.6% of the population had access to water supply (93% in urban areas), and 53.2% to sanitation services (61% in urban areas) (Figure 3.2 -in Portuguese) (SNIS, 2018[3]),.

Second, the characteristics of the water sector imply that it is highly sensitive to and dependent on multi-level governance (OECD, 2015[4]). This is further exacerbated in the context of a decentralised federation such as Brazil. In addition, there are a high number of sub-national regulatory agencies in WSS: a total of 72, including 34 municipal, 13 inter-municipal, and 25 state regulators. Therefore, there is a need for coordination between ANA, federal regulators, municipal/local governments, and the federal government.

Third, whilst the scope of ANA's responsibilities has expanded, especially with regard to the new matters of harmonisation (through the issuance of reference standards applicable to all sub-national authorities, as well as the oversight function over their implementation), shortcomings in its mandate are noted, especially in relation to its lack of enforcement powers.

Figure 3.2. Water and Sanitation data – a snapshot for Brazil (2018)

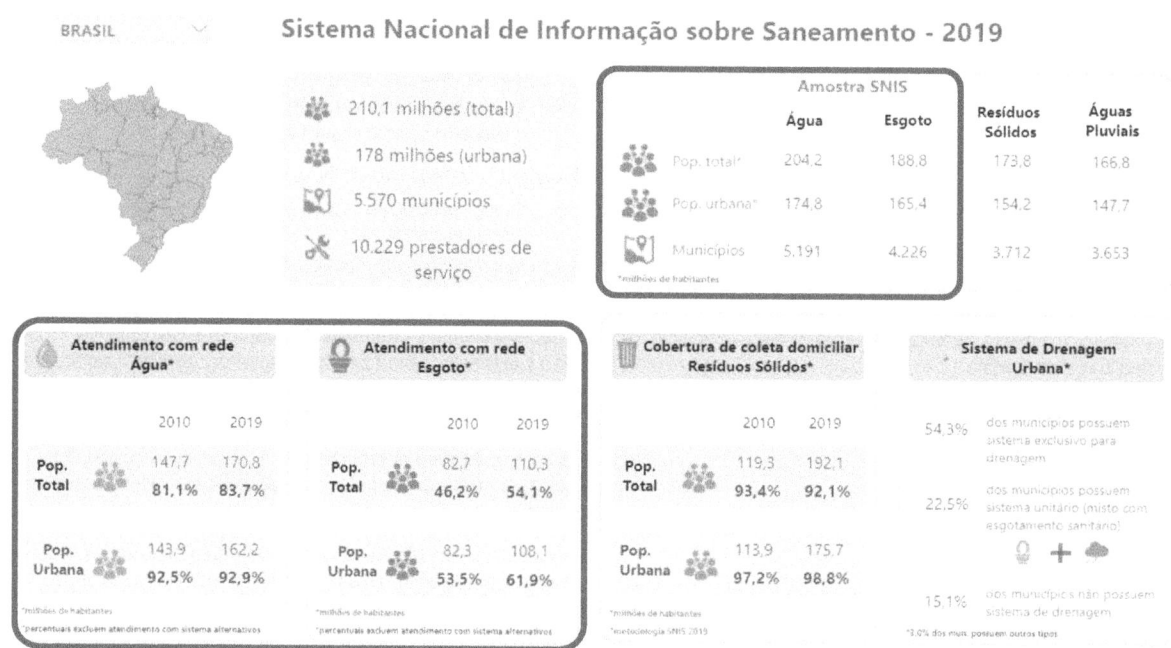

Source: SNIS (2018[3]), *The National Sanitation Information System*, http://www.snis.gov.br/painel-informacoes-saneamento-brasil/web/painel-setor-saneamento.

Making the reform effective

According to international practices and OECD normative frameworks, some key dimensions should be taken into account by ANA for the successful delivery of the new national framework and legislation. The proposals are described below.

Achieving role clarity

The reform of Brazil's water and sanitation sector is an ambitious undertaking and its success rests on the collaborative effort and effective coordination of all actors. The new regulatory framework defined in the Sanitation Law provides for long term goals (i.e.: December 2033 for the achievement of universal provision of WSS).

At the same time, the framework implies that a high number of actors need to be involved for the framework's successful delivery. As outlined in Table 3.2, the current sector relationship matrix is complex, even when disregarding current and future customers, or investors: municipal, regional, and state authorities retain responsibility for the provision of services and development of local regulation, with federal authorities looking after national regulation, as well as planning and funding infrastructure.

Table 3.2. WSS framework and actors involved

Activity	Actors responsible			
	Municipal authorities	Regional/inter-municipal authorities	State authorities	Federal authorities
Service provision	X	X	X	
Development of regulation	X	X	X	X (ANA)
Infrastructure planning	X	X		X
Funding of infrastructure			X	X

Source: Official Journal of the Union (2020[1]), *Law 14.026 of 15 July 2020*, https://www.in.gov.br/en/web/dou/-/lei-n-14.026-de-15-de-julho-de-2020-267035421; ANA (2021[2]), *Homepage*, https://www.ana.gov.br/eng/ (accessed on 20 November 2021); OECD/ANA (2019-21[5]), "Water Governance Workshops".

The South Australian regulator, the Essential Services Commission of South Australia (ESCOSA), was in a similar position to ANA while receiving additional responsibilities because of regulatory reform. Similarly to ANA, ESCOSA operates in a federal system (however without federal oversight) and is impacted by a number of layers of governance. To achieve role clarity and define responsibilities for all actors involved in the new regulatory make-up, ESCOSA and the other sector actors created a series of high-level pacts ("relationship agreements"). Through those, the relevant actors understood each other's short- and long-term objectives driven by the reform, and were able to act in sync for the achievement of the new policy objectives (ESCOSA, 2020[6]). In addition, such high-level pacts can become useful operational tools and be referred to as needed if dialogue or cooperation between actors goes off track.

An effective regulator must have clear objectives, with clear and linked functions and mechanisms to coordinate with other relevant bodies to achieve the desired regulatory outcomes. OECD *Best Practice Principles on the Governance of Regulators* describes how regulators can have a well-defined mission and distinct responsibilities within regulatory schemes. As OECD (2014[7]) states:

> *Unless clear objectives are specified, the regulator may not have sufficient context to establish priorities, processes and boundaries for its work. In addition, clear objectives are needed so others can hold the regulator accountable for its performance.*

The strategic framework, including the vision, mission, and strategic objectives of the regulator offers an opportunity for the definition and communication of roles, responsibilities and expectations. Such exercises facilitate engagement of stakeholders in a discussion on the strategic direction of the regulator, while at the same time it is considered good practice that economic regulators have independence in defining their long-term strategies. OECD data shows that in the water sector, 70% of regulators received inputs from the government in the process of setting their strategy (OECD, 2018[8]). Such collaboration is especially relevant in the current Brazilian context, with the implementation of such a significant reform in water and sanitation services. The final strategic framework will need to be communicated to stakeholders in a transparent manner, possibly through a communications strategy that can include an updated website for ANA, and effective monitoring of strategic objectives.

In the case of ANA, the regulator must also manage potentially conflicting functions of water resources management and economic regulation of WSS (i.e., the performance of one function could potentially limit, or appear to compromise the regulator's ability to fulfil its other function). Such arrangements where a regulator is working on different public interests require good regulatory practices. Therefore, having institutional arrangements that ensure transparency in decision-making, accountability of decisions and actions are crucial. ESCOSA has gone through numerous changes in mandate over the past decade.

ESCOSA's experience suggests that clear regulatory objectives, coupled with robust internal governance and focus on creating good internal culture and values yield benefits in the long term.

Similar to Brazil, the European Union (EU) is a vast territory formed of 27 members with a very varied local geography, socio-economic priorities and consumer needs. Nonetheless, the EU has succeeded in introducing a common framework for the quality of water resources across all its members, while taking account of regional specificities. This is achieved through different legislative vehicles (directives and regulations), which set common principles (for example: recovery of costs, or the obligation for polluters to pay for the environmental harm they generate) and specific objectives (like on drinking-water quality standards, wastewater treatment, sludge disposal, etc.), while at the same time allowing EU members flexibility in application. In addition, data from the association of water regulators in the EU (Box 3.2) shows a wide scope of action among regulators.

As can be seen from the example of ARERA in Italy, the independence of a regulator (including financial, human resources and internal organisational aspects), is a key asset in enabling it to deliver its regulatory scope of action, as shown by the areas of the independence of ARERA (Box 3.1). In addition, similar to ANA, ARERA has gone through a change in functions in the past decade, which prompted it to reshape its regulatory approach to deliver the national policy for WSS.

Box 3.1. Independent regulation in Italy

The scope of action of the independent Italian regulator, ARERA is supported by a culture of independence.

Table 3.3. Scope of action and independence of ARERA

Scope of action of ARERA	Independence of ARERA
Economic regulation • definition of tariff methodology • tariff approval (including capital investment plans) • definition of service quality standards • unbundling of operators' accounts • consumer protection **Enforcement** • infringement and sanctioning procedures • Data collection and monitoring • inspections Information and institutional advising powers	• Board nomination procedure (Government, Parliament and qualified majority voting) • Board mandate (7 years) beyond Parliamentary cycle (5 years) • Financial autonomy (through tariffs, no state contributions) • Organizational autonomy (no interference by ministries) • High technical skills of Board and staff (economics, law, engineering) • Incompatibility of roles between the regulator and regulated actors • Binding acts, with no further legislation needed

Source: OECD/ANA (2019-21[5]), "Water Governance Workshops".

Box 3.2. European Water Regulators (WAREG) scope of regulatory action and independence

WAREG data suggests that regulatory agencies in the European Union have a wide scope of action, with responsibilities ranging from the setting of consumer standards and development of quality standards to data collection and tariff approval. This goes together with funding independence, with more than half of WAREG agencies receiving their main funding from the regulated companies.

Figure 3.3. Scope of regulatory action in WAREG

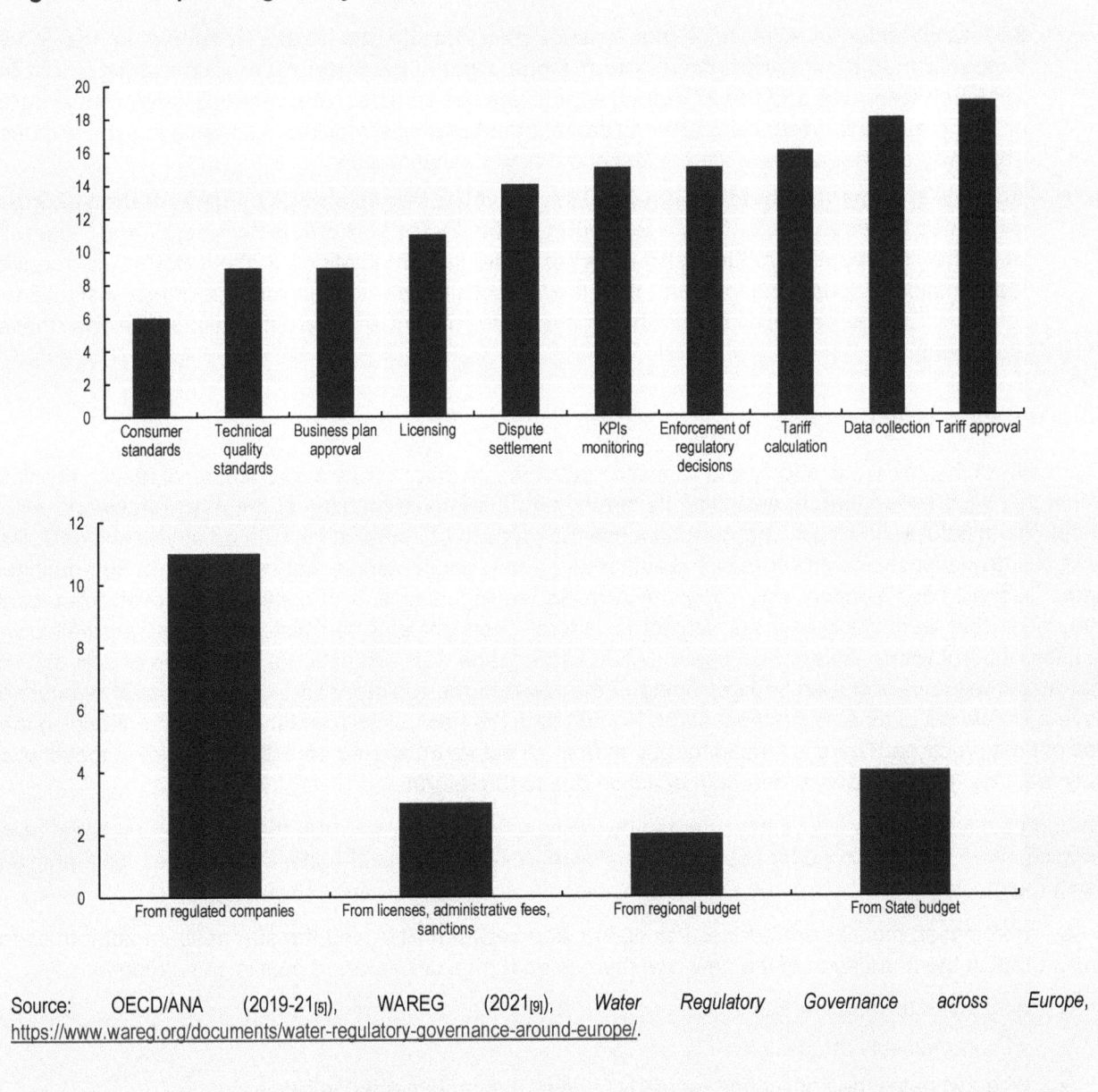

Source: OECD/ANA (2019-21[5]), WAREG (2021[9]), *Water Regulatory Governance across Europe*, https://www.wareg.org/documents/water-regulatory-governance-around-europe/.

The implementation of the new law will require:

- **Clear leadership by the Ministry of Regional Development and action by the Ministry of Economy, ANA, sub-national authorities, service providers, civil society and consumers.** Successful implementation of the reform rests on the collective effort of all actors and role clarity of each entity. In this ecosystem, it will be essential for ANA to define its new role regarding the reform and goals set by the government, and communicate this role, its responsibilities and areas of action to all stakeholders.

- **Relevant stakeholders to determine their ex-ante "definition of success".** More specifically, this should include realistic and attainable short- and long-term objectives and milestones for the stakeholders, as well as convergence areas for coordination among the stakeholders. The new legal and policy framework is a substantial undertaking that advances long-term goals. To this end, ANA should seek to build on its previous experience and draw realistic plans on what objectives are attainable in the short term, and which other goals require longstanding and multi-year work together with its stakeholders.
- **The facilitation by ANA of a higher-level pact among the actors involved in the WSS ecosystem, in a similar framework to the one created on water resources management in 2015 between ANA and the 27 states, which was based on conditionalities.** ANA should build on this previous experience in order to cement the basis of a regulatory scheme in sync with the objectives of other actors in the context of the new Sanitation Law.
- **Acknowledgement within the high-level pact that the reform and its implementation change dynamics between institutions intervening in the sector and create "winners" and "losers" in terms of responsibilities and powers.** The implementation of the reform will require identification of these changes and how they affect different stakeholders and inter-institutional relations. Engagement and capacity-building activities may need to be differentiated between these institutions.

Coordinating effectively

The reality of the new water supply and sanitation policy is that there will be a reallocation of responsibilities within the WSS ecosystem. In designing its strategy for the implementation of the new framework, ANA should be mindful of how such changes influence the process of coordination with other stakeholders. As ANA builds relationships with sub-national authorities, it may encounter resistance to change. Sub-national authorities will need to adopt and follow the ANA-issued regulations, and control is removed from local authorities that were previously not subject to federal oversight and had historically defined their own regulatory frameworks. A key challenge for ANA is to engage with sub-national authorities effectively, so that all parties have a shared understanding of the law and the regime, and that sub-national regulators have a simple set of tools to get them started in adopting the new reference standards and enhancing the use of best practices. There is a need for buy-in from all actors on shared objectives, including those who may feel they lost autonomy or freedom of action due to the reform.

Through the legal and policy context created by the new framework, and with the aid of international best practice, there is great scope for cooperation between ANA and the sub-national authorities, as identified using the guiding framework of the OECD Principles on Water Governance (Box 3.3).

A key coordination mechanism will need to be in place between ANA and the sub-national authorities to ensure that in the application of the new law, there is no formal or perceived conflict in relation to:

- who takes the final decision
- who implements the decision
- who evaluates the impact and regularly reviews the implementation process.

> **Box 3.3. Developing effective coordination following the OECD Principles on Water Governance**
>
> The OECD Principles on Water Governance (OECD, 2015[10]) provide a toolkit for developing effective coordination. Applied to the Brazilian context using the 2017 unpublished paper on the Governance of Drinking Water and Sanitation Infrastructure in Brazil (OECD, 2017[11]), the following can be outlined:
>
> 1. Effectiveness:
>   a. There is a need for coordination of municipal sanitation plans with national, state and regional policies.
>   b. There is a need for horizontal coordination and a clear prioritisation of targets at the federal level across programmes for grant funding in sanitation.
>   c. Information about the number of municipal supply systems in Brazil needs to be consolidated.
>   d. There is a need for a more consolidated approach, in comparison to the current fragmentation of responsibilities and programmes among federal authorities.
> 2. Efficiency:
>   a. There is a need for technical, planning and implementation capacity in municipalities.
>   b. Quality control needs to be implemented.
>   c. Financing matters, such as the ability to spend funds allocated, economic sustainability, lack of public confidence, entry of private investment, need to be addressed at the sub-national level.
> 3. Trust and engagement:
>   a. There are concerns about conflicts of interest at the municipal level.
>   b. There is weak participation of stakeholders and consumers.
>
> Source: OECD (2017[11]), *Report on the Governance of Drinking Water and Sanitation Infrastructure in Brazil*, https://www.ana.gov.br/todos-os-documentos-do-portal/documentos-sas/arquivos-cobranca/documentos-relacionados-saneamento/governance-of-ws-infrastructure-in-brazil_final.pdf.

This complements the regulatory approach examples from Italy at ARERA and from Australia at ESCOSA, where changes in the regulators' mandate prompted renewed coordination and dialogues with other national actors and industry. Effective coordination can be achieved through several key activities:

- ANA needs to engage with sub-national authorities so that all parties have a shared understanding of the law and the regime. For this, the OECD Principles on Water Governance as applied to the Brazilian context need to be considered. More specifically, there needs to be horizontal coordination at the federal level so that the various programmes for grant funding are aligned. There is a need for consolidation in approach among the federal authorities, and quality control needs to be implemented in a harmonised manner.
- ANA can facilitate a dialogue with other state authorities, including the sub-national regulators, so that the responsibilities of each agency are understood. Beyond increasing awareness, the sector actors need to be committed to the delivery of the new framework.

Defining an adequate transition period and managing expectations of ANA

A timing difference will arise between the passing of the new Sanitation Law and the development of reference standards by ANA, as well as the adoption of the regulations by sub-national authorities. At the time of the workshops (October 2020), ANA already published the timetable of consultation and the prioritisation list for the development of the reference standards (ANA, 2020[12]).

In the process of developing regulations, and especially in this transition period, ANA should appraise its status quo. This can come in the form of a "gap exercise", though which ANA identifies on the one hand areas of regulation that work adequately in sub-national authorities and can thus be adapted for national scale-up very quickly, and on the other hand areas that need significant improvement and need an overhaul.

The new Sanitation Law is a long-term process, which represents a major overhaul from the previous framework in WSS. Therefore, it raised high expectations with the public and key stakeholders. Most of these fall to ANA, being the institution at the centre of the reform. Therefore, there is a need for ANA to deliver early successes, or "quick wins" in the first one or two years following the entry into force of the new law to show stakeholders the positive changes which stem from the reform. For this, the pilot projects (such as the upcoming water and sewage concession project in Alagoas) are important as they will set the tone in relation to how the framework can be put into practice.

In addition, the transition period will bring specific challenges that ANA, the federal government as finance provider and the sub-national authorities will need to manage. For instance, the vast majority of current contracts are concluded under the legal framework, and some have significant deficiencies. These contracts will need to be given special consideration. Also, a few contracts are expected to be signed in the immediate period after the passing of the new Sanitation Law. Although the reference standards are not finalised, specific objectives or principles need to be developed by ANA so that the new contracts are compliant with the new framework and good practice that is aimed to be adopted in Brazil.

Furthermore, ANA will need to be mindful of the legal precedent from the local legislature or state courts. Some of these might not be compatible with the reference standards that ANA intends to set, and ANA together with sub-national authorities will need a strategy to manage eventual discrepancies in the transition period.

ANA needs to manage the expectations which arise from its role as a standard-setter – more specifically in relation to the quality of regulation at the local level, which is expected to increase, not only through uniformity but through the sharing and infusion of good practice into sub-national authorities. Finally, ANA is once-removed from the service providers in its role as supervisor of state regulators (as local regulators will supervise the providers), and the success of the final desired outcomes will rest on constructive and effective relations between the federal and state regulators.

In sum, managing the transition period will require:

- An assessment by ANA of the status quo across all sub-national authorities, as well as an appraisal of current adequate standards and practices at some sub-national authorities.
- ANA should take a clear stance in managing expectations in the short term in relation to what can be delivered for the consumers and the sector in the next couple of years, as well as how the provision and the contractual practicalities will be dealt with until the reference standards have been developed and implemented.

Building adequate human and technical capacities

ANA is regarded by stakeholders as professional, mature and well-respected. The addition of new responsibilities through the 2020 Sanitation Law came as recognition of its previous capacity and success in the area of water resources management. To implement the reform, the new mandate and functions must be accompanied by an effort to ensure funding, skills and competences, as well as unified culture.

Current skills within ANA do not necessarily fit the new functions. At the moment, ANA has adequate human resources for water resources management. The new responsibilities in relation to the regulation of WSS (issuing of reference standards and oversight, capacity building, relationship building, etc.) require focusing on a different set of skills. Usually, staff of water regulators requires expertise from the economics, accounting and legal professions (Figure 3.4).

Aside from an assessment of the skills needed, the fiscal situation in Brazil means that ANA will encounter difficulties to update its workforce given stringent federal rules. The Brazilian Ministry of Economy enforces the rules around recruitment and headcount, with the requirement that public agencies file a request for public exams with the Ministry of Economy to recruit personnel for professional positions. Such positions will make up the bulk of ANA's workforce needed for the delivery of the new mandate. Historically, the Ministry of Economy authorised a few public exams for public agencies with the justification of maintaining fiscal balance. Although federal restrictions on career progression based on experience and academic training, and salary increases in line with the length of service have been lifted, other restrictions, such as on movement of personnel across agencies (Government of Brazil, 2018[13]) remain.

Figure 3.4. Job families in water regulatory agencies

% of job families and professions represented in selected regulatory agencies

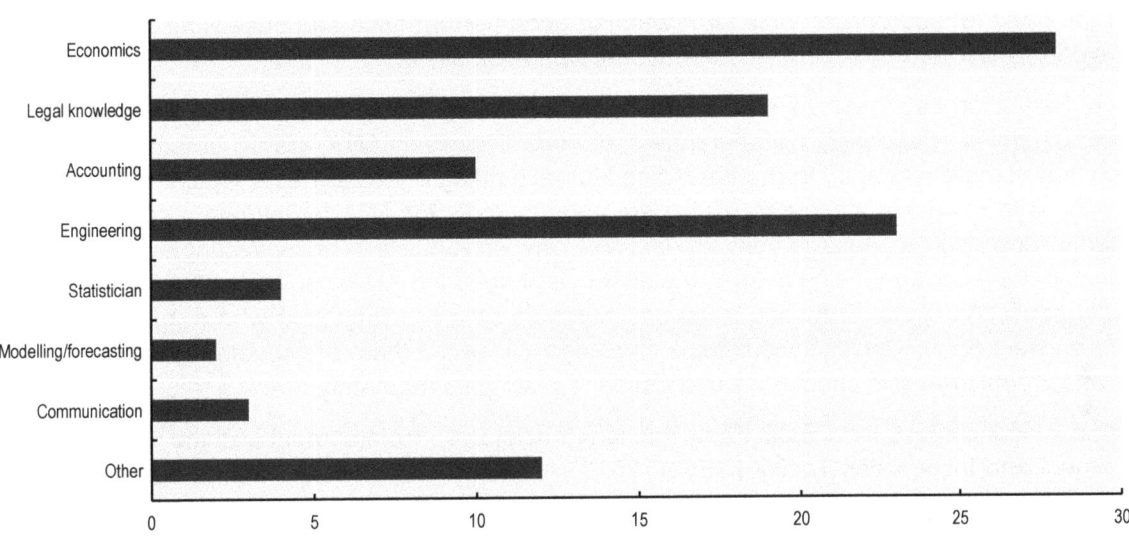

Note: Based on OECD Survey on the Governance of Water Regulators (2014).
Source: OECD (2015[14]), *The Governance of Water Regulators*, Paris, https://doi.org/10.1787/9789264231092-en.

In sum, the following solutions can be considered:

- At the moment, ANA has adequate human resources for water resources management. The new responsibilities in relation to the regulation of WSS (issuing of reference standards and oversight, capacity building, relationship building, etc.) require a focus on a different set of skills. Therefore, it is advisable that ANA not focus only on the substance of the regulatory reform, but also on the internal management and resources needed for the delivery of early successes. For instance, ANA will need to rethink its skills set and add more legal, economics and data analytics specialists to an already well-established engineering-focused staff base. Integrating new professionals into ANA will likely be a challenge since current professionals will have to "make room" for additions. Further, the various disciplines will need to work together to add maximum value to ANA's decision-making and regulatory processes, rather than competing internally.
- ANA should be mindful of the additional financial resources needed to carry out the mandate bestowed by the new Sanitation Law, as well as consider how the increased financial burden will be resourced, and how this might affect its independence in the long term.

Achieving effective oversight and enforcement

The new Sanitation Law tasks ANA with the responsibility of overseeing the adoption of and adherence to the new WSS reference standards by the sub-national authorities. However, the new function is not accompanied by corresponding enforcement powers, which is at odds with OECD best practice recommendations that "all key regulatory functions are discharged by responsible authorities with enforcement powers". This suggests that ANA has a narrow scope of action when it comes to its regulations. However, it can develop a benchmarking system that presents performance comparisons. The increase in transparency can put pressure on actors that are not implementing reference standards.

OECD data from the survey on the Governance of Regulators (OECD, 2014[7]) suggests that among the five economic sectors, the scope of action of water regulators is the second least restricted. The scope of action refers to the range of activities that the regulator can perform, including decision-making, enforcement and sanctioning powers. Instead of enforcement mechanisms, the new law creates indirect incentives for sub-national authorities to adapt ANA-issued WSS regulations – notably that the federal government will provide municipalities with access to federal funding for WSS contingent upon the adoption of the regulations issued by ANA by the sub-national regulatory agencies. From an interactive polling on Day 3 of the second workshop session, it emerged that by an overwhelming majority the participants viewed the need for appropriate tools for rewarding good performance and penalising poor performance as a top priority tool for ANA to deliver the national sanitation strategy.

The new Sanitation Law bestows onto ANA the responsibility to regularly review the progress of sub-national authorities in adopting the reference standards. However, ANA has no enforcement powers to sanction non-compliance, apart from withholding federal funding from state level regulators in case of non-compliance with reference standards. There are no legal tools for ANA to develop a compliance-driven, incremental approach to enforcement. In addition, the current state of play suggests that municipal authorities have received funding even in the absence of adopting ANA-issued regulations and designing municipal sanitation plans. Enforcing rules and pursuing policy in a context where implementation and supervision were previously lax constitutes a challenge. However, there are several approaches that ANA can develop to mitigate this structural shortcoming regarding its regulatory powers.

Even in this legal context, the OECD Best Practice Principles on Enforcement and the OECD Regulatory Enforcement and Inspections Toolkit (OECD, 2018[15]) offer ANA guidance on developing a strategy for the performance of effective inspections. The aims of a good enforcement system are to:

- Deliver the best possible outcomes in terms of risk prevention or mitigate and promote economic prosperity, enhance welfare and pursue the public interest.
- Ensure trust and satisfaction among different stakeholders, whose perspectives often conflict (OECD, 2012[16]). This is important in the current Brazilian context, where roles, responsibilities and functions of different sub-national authorities and local providers might change long-term while implementing the new WSS framework.

Even in the absence of enforcement powers, ANA can and should use a suite of "soft approach" tools to increase the likelihood that sub-national authorities become more compliant with ANA-issued regulations. These are:

- **Engaging with the sub-national agencies.** This is explained in detail in section "stakeholder engagement" below. ANA's role will be crucial in making the relevant WSS sector actors involved in a meaningful way in the process of setting the reference standards.
- **Strengthening and building capacity.** Providing capacity-building to sub-national WSS regulatory agencies is one of the ANA's main new responsibilities that can be leveraged to support state regulators' compliance with new regulatory requirements. To discharge the duty of capacity-building successfully, ANA needs to start by assessing the current skills and gaps in knowledge or

skills at state regulators. In this manner, it can identify good practices to share between state regulators and identify priority areas in the short term and develop a longer-term strategy.

- **Increasing transparency**. On one hand, transparency needs to be implemented in the functioning of the WSS sector (i.e., visibility of contracts, bid documents, performance indicators and progress against them, etc.). On the other hand, ANA's analyses and performance assessments on sub-national authorities' compliance with the reference standards (via a benchmarking system), as well as forward-looking strategies and stakeholder engagement plans/outcomes need to be made accessible in the public domain and written in a language that is accessible to specialised stakeholders and the wider public alike.

- **Collecting data and reporting to ANA.** There is a need for goals and targets for service providers (for instance, verifiable and clear thresholds that ANA receives). These should be codified in the reference standards and will need to include pre-set regulatory outcomes. ANA should also consider an array of means through which it receives information, including making use of current systems, such as the National Information System for Sanitation (SNIS). As noted from the example below (Box 3.4) at the Australian regulator, ESCOSA, the iterative regulatory model implies the use of a range of data and varied information for the regulator to perform ex-post analysis of the regulation. Similarly, the European Union carries out "fitness checks" to ensure that previous legislation is fit-for-purpose, and the result of the checks are taken into consideration as part of the broader legislative impact assessments in the water sector (EC, 2020[17]). In addition, the Italian national independent regulator, ARERA, employs a site of data-gathering powers to support its regulatory and enforcement actions.

Finally, ANA can explore the development and use of new approaches based on the principles of "responsive regulation". In other words, enforcement action should be modulated depending on the profile and behaviour of specific businesses. However, from a behavioural perspective, a sanction-led approach has shown to be ineffective at deterring poor behaviour and is premised on the faulty assumption that market actors are likely to misbehave. In fact, research shows that only a small number of people intentionally do bad things. Research further shows that most people want to do the right thing most of the time but might not know what or how to do it. Therefore, what is needed is help to do the right thing (Hodges, 2017[18]). This is the core of Ethical Business Regulation (EBR).

EBR draws on the findings of behavioural psychology, shared ethical values, and economic and cultural incentives, and starts from the core idea that decisions are made by people, rather than organisations. EBR implies a collaborative approach to the development and implementation of regulation, and implies dialogue between market actors, their stakeholders and public officials based on a shared ethical approach. In the absence of enforcement powers, the application of EBR elements in the oversight and regulatory process can be a strategy that ANA employs. EBR was embraced by the Water Industry Commission for Scotland in the process of future charges review, and allowed the regulator to reshape not only its approach to regulation but also its relationship with key stakeholders, including industry and consumers (Box 3.5). ANA can look at adopting EBR principles in the development of its reference standards, as well as in devising its stakeholder engagement strategy, which is further discussed in sub-section "Ensuring effective stakeholder engagement".

Box 3.4. ESCOSA Business Model

The ESCOSA business model presupposes an iterative approach to regulation, whereby performance and evaluations are defined at the end of the regulatory cycle. Therefore, regulations are reviewed in light of the regulator's strategy, so that they remain relevant and allow ESCOSA to deliver in line with its mandate.

Figure 3.5. ESCOSA business model

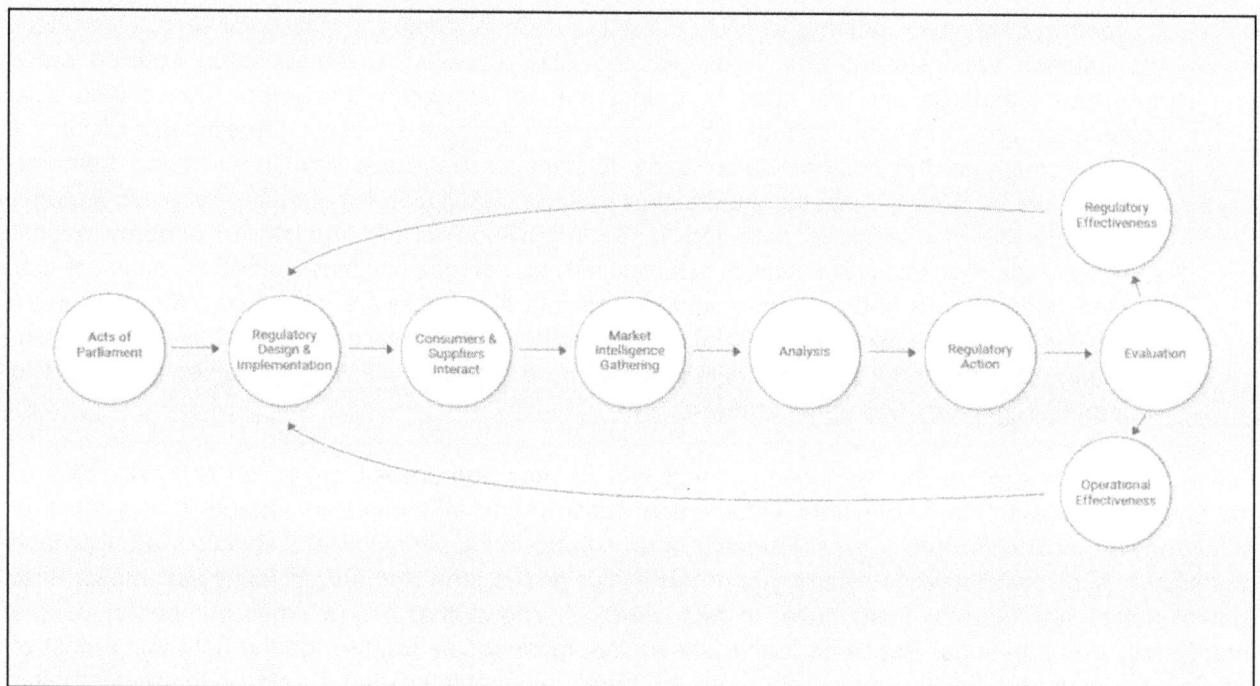

ESCOSA has a long-term objective defined as "the protection of the long-term interests of South Australian consumers with respect to the price, quality and reliability of essential services", which is defined by legislation. On this, the regulator built its purpose statement of adding "long-term value to the South Australian community by meeting its objective through its independent, ethical and expert regulatory decisions and advice". In its strategy document, ESCOSA goes further and defines the values which will enable it to achieve its statutory objective, and thus guide its regulatory activities: responsiveness, accountability, innovation and the building of inclusive relationships.

Source: ESCOSA (2021[19]), *Strategy 2021-2024*, https://www.escosa.sa.gov.au/about-us/strategic-plans.

Box 3.5. Ethical Based Regulation at WICS, UK

The Water Commission Industry for Scotland has been reviewing its charges for water for the period 2021-2027. In doing so, WICS worked closely with water industry stakeholders to put in place the key elements of a new regulatory approach, which focuses on establishing the best outcomes for customers, communities and the environment.

> In particular, stakeholders have committed to adopting the principles of Ethical Business Regulation (EBR), which requires open and honest conversations about the future challenges for the Scottish water industry and how best to tackle them. Transparency was determined as paramount in all interactions between the regulator, the providers of services and other stakeholders (including the public and consumers).
>
> Source: WICS (2020[20]), *Strategic Review of Charges*, https://www.watercommission.co.uk/UserFiles/Documents/VB2140%20WICS%20Methodology%20update_8.1.pdf; WICS (2020[21]), *Strategic Review of Charges 2021-27 – Draft Determination*, https://www.watercommission.co.uk/UserFiles/Documents/Strategic%20Review%20of%20Charges%202021-27%20Draft%20Determination_1.pdf.

Several solutions can be devised for achieving oversight in the absence of enforcement powers at ANA:

- ANA should ensure that the rules around the allocation of funding for authorities that did not follow the reference standards are enforced. Such actions demonstrate the robustness of the framework and set the tone for how the new policy is to be pursued.
- Even without enforcement powers, a suite of soft tools can be implemented by ANA, as follows:
  - maintaining continuous and meaningful engagement with the sub-national agencies
  - strengthening and building capacity at sub-national WSS regulatory agencies
  - enhancing transparency in decision-making and in the functioning of WSS
  - establishing a robust system of data collection, analysis and reporting.
- ANA should consider the development of alternative, behaviourally driven approaches to the development of regulation, such as EBR, which implies a collaborative approach and dialogue between market actors, their stakeholders and public officials, based on a shared ethical approach.

Ensuring effective stakeholder engagement

In the process of stakeholder engagement, ANA should be mindful of the stakeholder groups it needs to engage with and define their role in this process since several different categories will need to be included. These are:

- the government, as the actor that defines the legal framework and national WSS strategy
- operators and sub-national agencies (including the employee groups such as syndicates and unions) as providers of services
- consumers, both current and future, which the national policy aims to affect

For this process to be successful, as the OECD normative framework (OECD, 2020[22]) suggests, there might be a need for ANA to educate stakeholders about engagement culture: stakeholders need to be informed about when and why they have a chance to influence the regulatory process. This would be especially relevant for smaller sub-national authorities that did not go through an engagement process before, or for newly established consumer groups created to address actors in the new system.

As a feature of stakeholder engagement, ANA should develop strategic partnerships as channels to share good practices to get to the core of the issues faced by sub-national authorities and provide insight and guidance where needed most. This, in turn, can help with the building of capacity. Through building capacity, ANA can also influence the relationship with consumers by empowering service providers to communicate better with the end-user (current or potential) (Figure 3.6). Note that unserved (potential) customers often lack voice in regulatory processes since they are usually the most vulnerable populations. ANA can provide incentives that help agencies address the long-term impacts of current policies.

Figure 3.6. Stakeholder process triangle

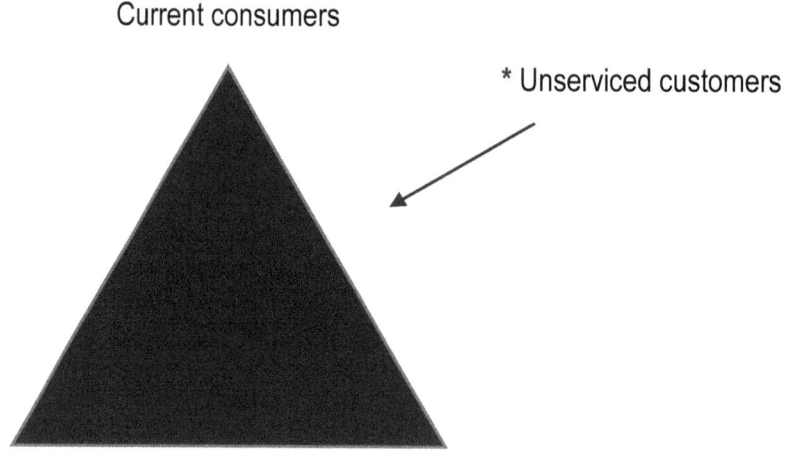

Source: OECD/ANA (2019-21[5]), "Water Governance Workshops".

As a particular characteristic of the Brazilian situation, ANA should also rethink its strategic relationship with the unions, associations, local regulatory agencies, public companies, etc. as component stakeholders of the sub-national authorities. Resistance to change from staff working in sub-national authorities or service providers can be exacerbated by the wider economic context (such as the current COVID-19 crisis) and fears over job loss. At ESCOSA, it is not unusual for the regulators to include a wide range of stakeholders in their formal engagement strategy. The advantage of engaging with a wide base of stakeholders is not only to enhance understanding of and compliance with the rules and regulations, but also to raise awareness of the activities of the regulator and increase public acceptance. Of course, establishing a track record of successful initiatives is crucial for the creation of trust among the citizenry.

Moreover, WSS is a capital-intensive and monopolistic sector, with important market failures. Thus, it is important for ANA to ensure that relevant stakeholders within this system of multi-level governance (including other federal regulators, federal and local governments) are continuously appraised of the regulatory developments in the sector. This means that stakeholder engagement and communication strategy is not only defined for the short term. Rather, it is advised to build and maintain a long-term relationship and culture of continual coordination, so that the objectives stated in the new Sanitation Law are achieved over the next decade.

In addition, the reality of the new framework is that, on one hand, the rules developed under the reference standards will be numerous and complex, recognising various inter-dependencies. On the other hand, ANA will have a high number of sub-national authorities whose regulation needs to be reviewed. This means that ANA will be disadvantaged in terms of knowledge and access to information. For this, a different approach to stakeholder engagement might need to be considered: like the high-level pacts with governing actors referred to in "Achieving role clarity", there is the possibility of creating such mechanisms with the service providers. These mechanisms are akin to a "moral contract", a commitment between the regulator and the regulated entities to work together in a spirit of trust, cooperation and open communication – with the aim to provide quality service to consumers and achieve agreed objectives (ESCOSA, 2000[23]). The benefits of a high-level pact with service providers are a less adversarial relationship, improved use of resources, better planning, and improved productivity, all of which lead to improved quality of service. ESCOSA used high-level pacts with the industry, which were also accompanied by a joint review procedure – or "health checks". These can come in the form of a questionnaire that assesses the robustness of the relationship, followed by open discussion in which results are discussed and possible solutions for deficiencies in the relationship are put forward by both parties.

In sum, effective stakeholder engagement will rely on several key elements:

- Strengthening the stakeholder engagement strategy internally at ANA, and using OECD guidance to educate and build expectations with external stakeholders on matters shared for consultation.
- Rethinking ANA's strategic relationship with the groups not usually engaged (for instance unions, or unserved consumers), and building these relationships keeping in mind the current economic context and the specific challenges that these groups might encounter.
- Keeping continuous dialogue with stakeholders, so all key players (including the federal government, sub-national authorities, consumer groups and private providers) are apprised of developments in the sector as they happen and there is a "no surprise" relationship among the sector actors.

Decentralising to achieve better regulatory outcomes

A key opportunity provided by the new legislative framework is its provision for the creation of regional units (which should include at least one metropolitan area).[2] This allows for changes to be driven and implemented at a higher level than before, as sub-national authorities will be empowered to develop initiatives and attract investment at the regional rather than municipal level as was the case before the legislative reform.[3] The regionalisation is designed to serve a dual role: (1) redistributing funds from wealthy to poorer areas, (2) achieving economies of scale through the implementation of larger-scale projects. According to the new Sanitation Law, it is within the remit of ANA to promote the regionalisation of service provision.[4] This will be done through the development of reference standards and regulations.

The understanding is that the regionalisation is not yet determined, but that it will consider geographical and water basin landscapes rather than only political regional boundaries. In the context of Brazil, the process of regionalisation for the purposes of implementing the new WSS policy is important, as it can allow for the regulatory model to be put into the local context, and thus target specific needs of each region. The Brazilian case is very similar to Italy, where regionalisation was implemented in WSS since 1995 (Box 3.6).

Box 3.6. Regionalisation in Italy: ARERA case study on territorial aggregation by uniform catchment areas

In Italy, the regulator for energy, networks and environment, ARERA, is the independent authority that, since 1996, sets tariffs and service quality standards. ARERA also monitors their compliance and enforces the standards through penalties and rewards within the national legislative environmental framework. The regulatory competencies were initially designed to the break monopoly in gas and electricity transmission and distribution services, and were prompted by the liberalisation process in the energy sector and by EU legislation to reinforce the internal energy market. In 2012, these were extended by law to water and wastewater utility services to better implement national water policies set by the Italian government.

In terms of water sector governance, Italy introduced the concept of Optimal Territorial Entities (*Ambiti Territoriali Ottimali*, ATO) in 1994. These are single catchment areas defined within each of the 20 Italian regions. Each ATO is governed by an assembly formed of representatives of all the municipalities included in its jurisdiction, which takes fundamental decisions on the governance of the sector, such as:

- defining criteria to select service suppliers, according to EU laws (competition for the market)
- coordinating with service suppliers to collect and validate data required to set local tariffs, according to the methodology defined by ARERA at the national level
- defining objectives to be achieved and draft business plans to be approved by ARERA
- monitoring of the realisation of planned investment.

The progressive reduction in the number of ATOs in the past years, combined with the effects of ARERA's regulation, has reduced the extreme fragmentation of water services. Therefore, the number of operators decreased from more than 8,000 in the late 1990s to fewer than 2,100 today.

More specifically, ARERA's regulation has promoted:

- horizontal integration by creating economic incentives for the merger of operators within each ATO, and thus leading to economies of scale
- vertical integration of different water services (potable water, sanitation and sewage treatment) into a single service for economies of scope.

Figure 3.7. Multi-level water governance in Italy

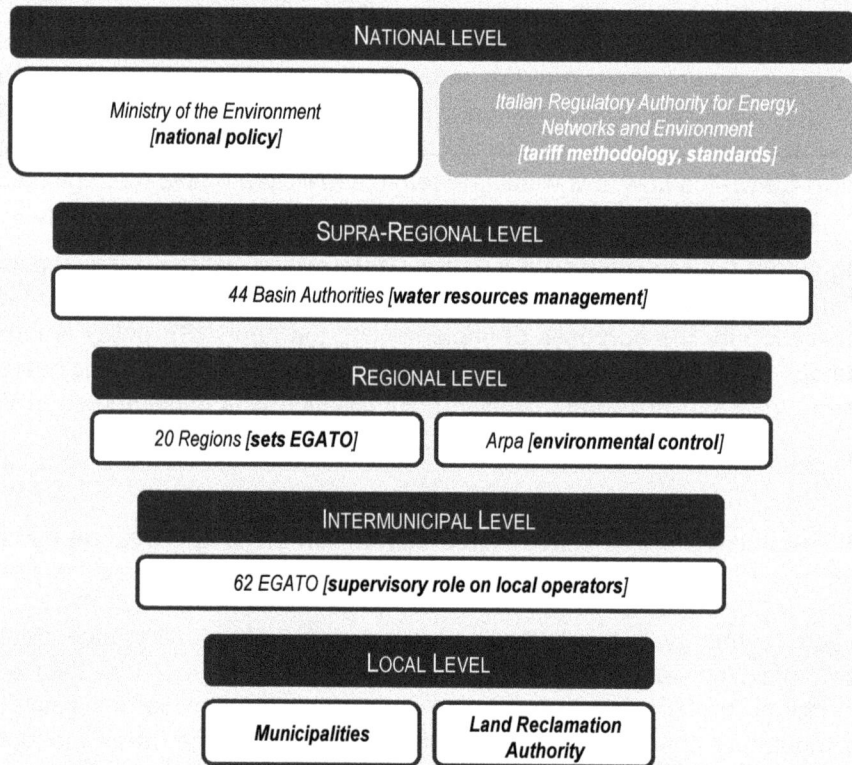

Regions decide which municipalities are aggregated in ATOs, with no involvement from the government or the national regulator. The Governing Entity of the ATO takes the decision on whether the service supplier should be selected through a tender (for fully private suppliers), or supplied in-house (for public suppliers) or by a public-private partnership (with the private partner selected through a tender). The local tariffs are approved by ARERA after a compliance check against the national tariff methodology, also defined by ARERA.

Source: OECD/ANA (2019-21[5]), "Water Governance Workshops"; Official Gazette of the Italian Republic (1994[24]), *Law n. 36/1994 (Galli Law)*, https://www.gazzettaufficiale.it/eli/id/1994/01/19/094G0049/sg.

In sum, to achieve the regionalisation objectives of the new law:

- ANA should work with the other relevant federal authorities for the successful definition and implementation of the regionalisation objectives of the new Sanitation Law, since ANA will be in the position of having a "helicopter view" of the WSS status quo and emerging opportunities.
- ANA should devise and promote policies which incentivise sub-national authorities to pursue investment projects from a regional, rather than local viewpoint. Particular attention should be given to the professionalisation of both regulators and operators.

Planning infrastructure and involving the private sector in WSS

OECD research shows that regulation plays an important role in investment through effects on determining the return on investment as well as ensuring efficient use and expansion of infrastructure through the effects of pricing (Cette, Lecat and Ly-Marin, 2017[25]) (OECD, 2017[26]). In particular, barriers to entry are found to influence investment negatively, and that regulatory independence is shown to boost investment when combined with incentive-based regulation.

In addition, the Survey on the Governance of Water Regulators (Figure 3.8) shows that increasing investment is a core part of the regulatory functions among water regulators. This is in line with the newly bestowed mandate of ANA.

Figure 3.8. Core regulatory functions carried out by water regulators

(Number of regulators/34)

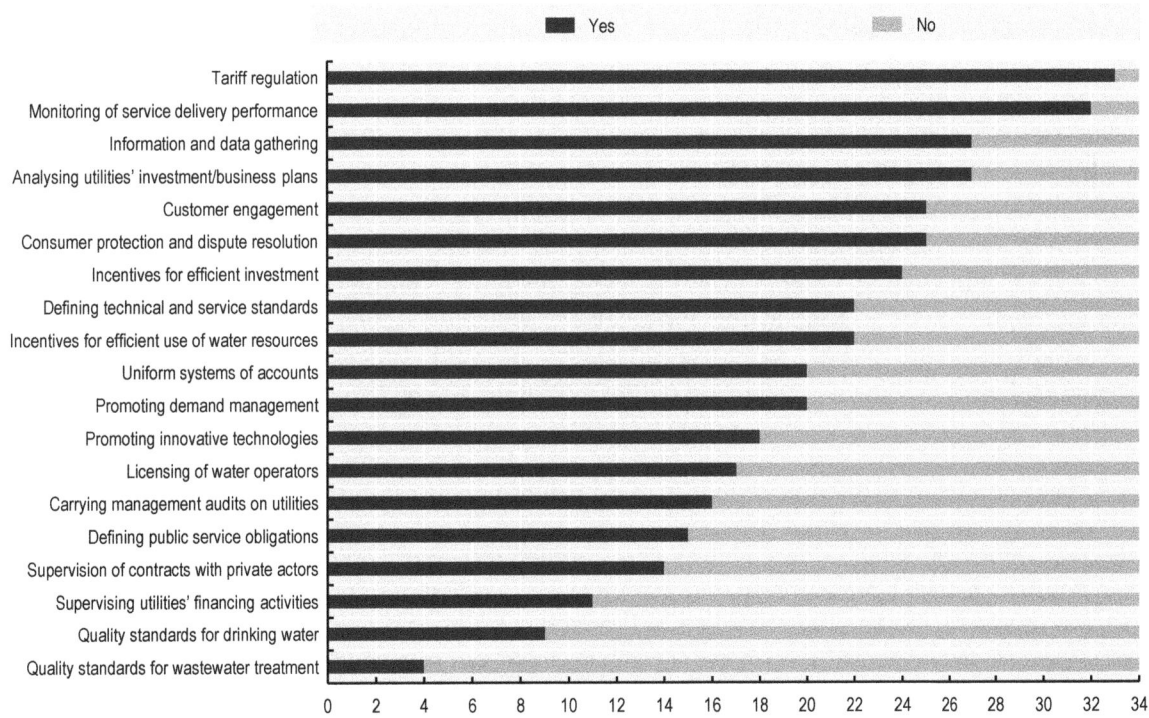

Note: Based on OECD Survey on the Governance of Water Regulators (2014)
Source: OECD (2015[14]), *The Governance of Water Regulators*, https://doi.org/10.1787/9789264231092-en.

The Recommendation on the Governance of Infrastructure (OECD, 2020[27]), adopted by the OECD Council in July 2020, provides countries with practical guidance for efficient, transparent and responsive decision-making processes in infrastructure investment. This comes in the form of 10 specific recommendations that are interdependent (Figure 3.9). The recommendations can be adapted to the Brazilian context as they support a whole-of-government approach and cover the entire life cycle of infrastructure projects, putting special emphasis on regional, social, gender and environmental considerations. A key feature is the promotion of a coherent, predictable and efficient regulatory network.

Figure 3.9. OECD Recommendation on the Governance of Infrastructure

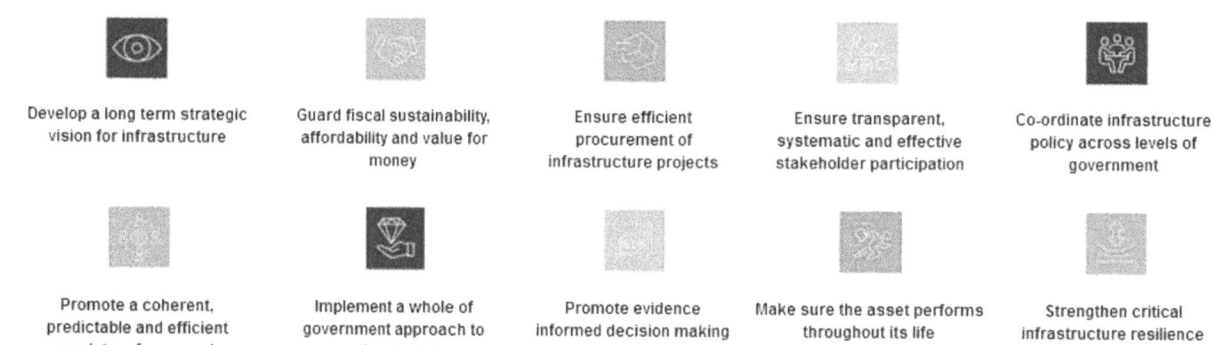

Source: OECD (2020[27]), *Recommendation of the Council on the Governance of Infrastructure*, https://legalinstruments.oecd.org/en/instruments/OECD-LEGAL-0460.

The Brazilian government has set targets for investment in WSS through the National Sanitation Plan. However, in addition to long-standing fiscal constraints, there is the newly emerged additional challenge which stems from the COVID-19 crisis. Therefore, infrastructure investment and delivery are important tools for the economic and social recovery efforts in the foreseen economic context. In practice, and in harmony with the objectives of the national policy on WSS, ANA needs to look at creating long-term incentives to attract private and foreign investors and, in some cases, to encourage existing companies to continue the provision of current services.

In addition to the guidelines provided by the legal framework and international practice, Brazil already has experience in opening network sectors to private investors. This happened in the electricity sector from the 1990s, and ANA should strive to learn from that experience (i.e., through research of privatisation policy and contracts, with knowledge sharing from the electricity regulator, *Agência Nacional de Energia Elétrica*). There is scope to create forums for cross-fertilisation between Brazilian sector regulators and their experiences and roles in the implementation of major reforms and ambitious policy goals.

Box 3.7. Lessons from ARERA about increasing private sector investment

Private involvement in WSS in Italy has been a controversial topic due to the public perception that water is a public good. This materialised in 2011 through a national referendum that ended mandatory competitive tendering for water concessions and ended the explicit requirement that firms receive a fair rate of return when water tariffs were set. In this context, the role of the national regulator, ARERA, became instrumental in the incentivisation of water infrastructure investments.

Currently, three main functions influence investment through ARERA's regulatory approach:

1. ARERA has the power to approve economic and financial plans of single operators (received through the governing entity of the ATOs) and to ask for modifications in case of non-compliance with the tariff methodology. ARERA can also impose sanctions in case data is not received or

> correctly modified; this increases the quality of information provided to the regulator and promotes stability in the water sector.
> 2. Through a single national tariff methodology (divided into variants that consider the diverse economic and financial situation of Italian regions), ARERA promotes efficient infrastructure and management planning, resulting in positive effects on investment development and infrastructure value.
> 3. ARERA's rules are defined every four years, with an update every two years. This brings certainty and stability in the sector, elements fundamental to attracting investment capital. This is done based on observed and measured costs, not as a consequence of political interference. It also lowers the risk of reviewing regulatory schemes, hence increasing the capability to program future investments.
>
> As a result of ARERA's regulatory approach, the level of investment in Italy has constantly risen: investments reached EUR 38.7/inhabitant in 2017, with a total increase of 24% from 2012 to 2018. For 2018-19, investments reached EUR 44.6/inhabitant.
>
> Between 2016 and 2019, investment expenditure (including the availability of public funds) amounted to EUR 11.9 billion (EUR 2.2 billion in 2016, EUR 2.8 billion in 2017, EUR 3.5 billion in 2018 and EUR 3.4 billion in 2019).
>
> Source: OECD/ANA (2019-21[5]), "Water Governance Workshops"; Official Gazette of the Italian Republic (2017[28]), *Law n.205/17*, https://www.gazzettaufficiale.it/eli/id/2017/12/29/17G00222/sg; ARERA (2019[29]), *Annual Report*, https://www.arera.it/it/inglese/annual_report/relaz_annuale.htm#.

The planning of infrastructure investment will be reliant on several key elements:

- The responsibility of ANA on the creation of reference standards should consider policies that incentivise the sub-national authorities to seek private investment. In this process, ANA can learn from other national agencies, such as the electricity regulator.
- In the context of ANA and of the new Sanitation Law, the OECD Recommendations on the Governance of Infrastructure can be applied using the following elements:
    - identifying policy goals, and evaluating whether regulation is necessary and how it can be most effective and efficient in achieving those goals
    - considering means other than regulation and identifying the trade-offs of the different approaches analysed to identify the best approach
    - supporting coordination between supranational, national and sub-national regulatory frameworks
    - providing evidence-based tools for regulatory decisions, including stakeholder engagement, economic, fiscal, social and environmental impact assessment, audit and ex post evaluation
    - conducting systematic reviews of existing regulation relevant to infrastructure, including consideration of costs and benefits, to ensure that regulations are up to date, cost justified, cost effective and consistent, and deliver the intended policy objectives
    - promoting good governance of regulatory agencies to ensure sustainable tariff setting, overall regulatory quality and confidence in the market, and contribute to the overall achievement of policy goals (e.g., independence, transparency, accountability, scope of action, enforcement, capacity and resourcing).

Understanding finance providers' perspectives

In addition to understanding the investment needs of specific regions, ANA and the other relevant actors in the WSS sector (including government) need to understand what specifics are needed by private investors and finance providers in the process of designing of a regulatory framework aimed at increasing incentives for private investment. For instance, key questions such as contracts funding, incentives of operators and sub-national authorities to keep to the terms of the agreement in the long term (30 years or more), and the availability of adequate financial products need to be considered.

Furthermore, as mentioned in the sub-section on Planning infrastructure and involving the private sector in WSSPlanning infrastructure and involving the private sector in WSS above, ANA's regulations and reference standards need to influence operators to seek private funding and not just look at sources of government funding, with a view to covering long-term costs and increasing investment efficiency.

Regulatory stability is an expected outcome from the issuance by ANA of reference standards and harmonisation of regulation among the sub-national authorities. This is a key characteristic that private investors look for. Therefore, for the sanitation policy to achieve its objective of increasing private access to WSS, there needs to be commitment to maintaining a harmonised framework and applying it to the new contracts. Otherwise, there is the risk that investors lose faith in the new framework and private capital will not be invested.

Public acceptance of private sector involvement

Public acceptance of private involvement in the WSS can present two issues. On one hand, as one of the international experts highlighted in the workshop, a feature of the current situation is that local politics is involved in the operation and provision of WSS by municipalities. Change of this status quo can be difficult, and ANA should work with the local authorities to highlight the benefits for consumers which arise from further investment and private sector involvement. As Professor Berg noted in the slide deck for workshop week 19-22 October, citizens "need to be confident that the system works for them".

On the other hand, there is a risk that there will be an initial cultural aversion by consumers to any increased private management of water services, stemming from the perception of water resources as a public good. Public acceptance of private sector involvement is important, as citizens' perceptions are fundamental to the accountability of regulation. ANA can look at several solutions. For instance, a dedicated economic regulator in charge of guaranteeing the public interest, such as Ofwat in England and Wales (UK), can achieve public confidence in a completely privatised industry, and ANA can look to position itself as being such a guarantor. Alternatively, public confidence might be maintained by ensuring transparent management arrangements with stakeholder involvement and a clear political lead in strategic decisions (for instance, by ensuring controlling public authority participation in the capital of any public-private partnership). Finally, learning from example at WICS, a collaborative approach with the wider public, can be achieved through a consultation process that puts the customers and communities at the heart of the process (this can be done through the form of customer consultation panels, consumer forums, etc.).

The following elements need to be considered:

- Dialogue among the relevant stakeholders, especially the providers of private finance, is needed to understand the challenges that the current framework poses for investors. This would highlight whether the financial framework is suited for the purposes and needs of WSS investment, and could flag further areas beyond WSS policy that the federal government needs to consider.
- The harmonisation and stability of the regulatory and WSS contractual framework brought by ANA's reference standards will be key in attracting new investment.

- Public acceptance of private investment in WSS will be noted both at the level of service provision, as well as by the end consumers. ANA should work on raising awareness among these stakeholder groups about the short- and long-term benefits of private investment.

References

ANA (2021), *Homepage*, Agência Nacional de Águas, https://www.ana.gov.br/eng/ (accessed on 2021 November 20). [2]

ANA (2020), *Agenda regulatória 2020-2021-2022*. [12]

ARERA (2019), *Annual Report*, https://www.arera.it/it/inglese/annual_report/relaz_annuale.htm#. [29]

Cette, G., R. Lecat and C. Ly-Marin (2017), "Long-term growth and productivity projections in advanced countries", *OECD Journal: Economic Studies*, Vol. 2016/1, https://dx.doi.org/10.1787/eco_studies-2016-5jg1g6g5hwzs. [25]

EC (2020), *EU Water Legislation - Fitness Check*, European Commission, https://ec.europa.eu/environment/water/fitness_check_of_the_eu_water_legislation/index_en.htm. [17]

ESCOSA (2021), *Strategy 2021-2024*, Essential Services Commission of South Australia, https://www.escosa.sa.gov.au/about-us/strategic-plans. [19]

ESCOSA (2020), *Regulators Working Group*, Essential Services Commission of South Australia, https://www.escosa.sa.gov.au/industry/water/retail-pricing/sa-water-regulatory-determination-2020/regulators-working-group. [6]

ESCOSA (2000), *Speech by Lewis W. Owens at the SA Power Briefing*, Essential Services Commission of South Australia. [23]

Government of Brazil (2018), *Diário Oficial da União - Portaria n° 193, de 3 de Julho de 2018*, http://www.in.gov.br/materia/-/asset_publisher/Kujrw0TZC2Mb/content/id/28503558/do1-2018-07-04-portaria-n-193-de-3-de-julho-de-2018-28503542 (accessed on 17 June 2020). [13]

Hodges, S. (2017), *Ethical Business Practice and Regulation*, Hart Publishing. [18]

OECD (2020), *OECD Recommendation on the Governance of Infrastructure*, OECD, Paris, http://www.oecd.org/gov/infrastructure-governance/recommendation/. [30]

OECD (2020), "Public consultation on the draft OECD Best Practice Principles on Stakeholder Engagement in Regulatory Policy", OECD, Paris, https://www.oecd.org/gov/regulatory-policy/public-consultation-best-practice-principles-on-stakeholder-engagement.htm. [22]

OECD (2020), *Recommendation of the Council on the Governance of Infrastructure*, https://legalinstruments.oecd.org/en/instruments/OECD-LEGAL-0460. [27]

OECD (2018), *OECD 2018 Database on the Governance of Sector Regulators*, OECD, Paris, http://www.oecd.org/regreform/regulatory-databases-and-indicators.htm. [8]

OECD (2018), *OECD Regulatory Enforcement and Inspections Toolkit*, OECD Publishing, Paris, https://dx.doi.org/10.1787/9789264303959-en. [15]

OECD (2018), *The Governance of Regulators*, OECD, Paris, https://www.oecd.org/gov/regulatory-policy/governance-of-regulators.htm. [31]

OECD (2017), *OECD Journal: Economic Studies*, OECD Publishing, OECD, https://www.oecd-ilibrary.org/economics/oecd-journal-economic-studies_19952856. [26]

OECD (2017), *Report on the Governance of Drinking Water and Sanitation Infrastructure in Brazil*, https://www.ana.gov.br/todos-os-documentos-do-portal/documentos-sas/arquivos-cobranca/documentos-relacionados-saneamento/governance-of-ws-infrastructure-in-brazil_final.pdf. [11]

OECD (2015), *OECD Principles on Water Governance*, OECD, Paris, https://www.oecd.org/cfe/regionaldevelopment/OECD-Principles-on-Water-Governance-en.pdf. [10]

OECD (2015), *The Governance of Water Regulators*, OECD Studies on Water, OECD Publishing, Paris, https://dx.doi.org/10.1787/9789264231092-en. [14]

OECD (2015), *Water Resources Governance in Brazil*, OECD Studies on Water, OECD Publishing, Paris, https://dx.doi.org/10.1787/9789264238121-en. [4]

OECD (2014), *The Governance of Regulators*, OECD Best Practice Principles for Regulatory Policy, OECD Publishing, Paris, https://dx.doi.org/10.1787/9789264209015-en. [7]

OECD (2012), *Recommendation of the Council on Regulatory Policy and Governance*, OECD Publishing, Paris, https://dx.doi.org/10.1787/9789264209022-en. [16]

OECD/ANA (2019-21), "Water Governance Workshops". [5]

Official Gazette of the Italian Republic (2017), *Law n.205/17*, https://www.gazzettaufficiale.it/eli/id/2017/12/29/17G00222/sg. [28]

Official Gazette of the Italian Republic (1994), *Law n. 36/1994*, https://www.gazzettaufficiale.it/eli/id/1994/01/19/094G0049/sg. [24]

Official Journal of the Union (2020), *Law 14.026 of 15 July 2020*, https://www.in.gov.br/en/web/dou/-/lei-n-14.026-de-15-de-julho-de-2020-267035421. [1]

SNIS (2018), *The National Sanitation Information System*, Sistema Nacional de Informações sobre Saneamento, http://www.snis.gov.br/painel-informacoes-saneamento-brasil/web/painel-setor-saneamento. [3]

WAREG (2021), *Water Regulatory Governance across Europe*, https://www.wareg.org/documents/water-regulatory-governance-around-europe/ (accessed on 5 January 2022). [9]

WICS (2020), *Strategic Review of Charges*, https://wics.scot/publications/price-setting/strategic-review-charges-2021-27/approach/2021-27-methodology-refinements. [20]

WICS (2020), *Strategic Review of Charges 2021-27 – Draft Determination*, https://wics.scot/publications/price-setting/strategic-review-charges-2021-27/determinations/2021-27-draft-determination. [21]

Annex 3.A. Action plan

The tables summarise the main actions presented in Chapter 3.

Annex Table 3.A.1. Making water and sanitation regulation in Brazil more effective

Achieve role clarity	Clear leadership from the Ministry of Regional Development and actions from the Ministry of Finance, ANA, sub national authorities, service providers, civil society actors and consumers. The successful implementation of the reform rests on the collective effort of all actors and role clarity of each entity is important for implementation
	The relevant stakeholders should determine their ex ante "definition of success". More specifically, this should include realistic and attainable short-term and long-term objectives and milestones of the stakeholders, as well as convergence areas for coordination among the stakeholders.
	ANA should build on the previous experience of the 2015 resources management pact in order to cement the basis of a regulatory scheme that is in sync with the objectives of other actors in the context of the new Sanitation Law.
Coordinate effectively	ANA needs to engage with sub-national authorities effectively, so that all parties have a shared understanding of the law and the regime. For this, the OECD Principles on Water Governance as applied to the Brazilian context need to be considered. More specifically, there needs to be horizontal coordination at federal level, so that the various programmes for grant funding are aligned, there is a need for consolidation in approach among the federal authorities, and quality control needs to be implemented in a harmonised manner.
	ANA can facilitate a dialogue with other state authorities, including the sub-national regulators, so that the responsibilities of each agency are understood. Beyond increasing awareness, the sector actors need to be committed to the delivery of the new framework.
Define an adequate transition period and manage expectations from ANA	An assessment by ANA of the current status quo across all sub-national authorities, as well as an appraisal of current adequate standards and practices at some sub-national authorities.
	ANA should take a clear stance in managing short term expectations in relation to what can be delivered for the consumers and the sector in the next couple of years, as well as how the provision and contractual practicalities will be dealt with until the reference standards have been developed and implemented.
Build adequate human and technical capacities	It is advisable that ANA not only focus on the substance of the regulatory reform, but also on the internal management and resources needed for the delivery. For instance, ANA will need to rethink its skills set and add more legal, economics and data analytics specialists to an established engineering-focused staff base.
	ANA should be mindful of the additional financial resources needed to carry out the mandate bestowed by the new Sanitation Law, as well as consider how the increased financial burden will be resourced, and how this might affect its independence in the long term.
Achieve effective oversight and enforcement	ANA should ensure that the rules are enforced regarding the allocation of funding for those authorities that do not follow the reference standards. This demonstrates robustness of the framework and sets the tone on how the new policy is to be pursued.
	Even without enforcement powers, a suite of soft tools can be implemented by ANA, as follows: • Continuously and meaningfully engaging with sub-national agencies. • Strengthening and building capacity at sub-national WSS regulatory agencies. • Enhancing transparency in decision-making and in the functioning of WSS. Collecting data and reporting.
	ANA should consider the development of alternative, behaviourally driven approaches to the development of regulation, such as Ethical Business Regulation, which implies a collaborative approach and dialogue between market actors, their stakeholders and public officials, based on a shared ethical approach.
Ensure effective stakeholder engagement	Strengthen the stakeholder engagement strategy internally at ANA, as well as use OECD guidance to educate and build expectations with external stakeholders on the matters that will be shared for consultation.
	Rethink ANA's strategic relationship with groups not usually engaged (e.g., unions, or unserved consumers), and build these relationships keeping in mind the economic context and specific challenges that these groups might encounter.
	Keep a continuous dialogue with the relevant stakeholders for all key players (including federal government, sub-national authorities, consumer groups and private providers) to be apprised of the developments in the sector as they happen, so that there is a "no surprise" relationship among the sector actors.
Decentralise to achieve better regulatory outcomes	ANA should work with the other relevant federal authorities for the successful definition and implementation of the regionalisation objectives of the new Sanitation Law since ANA will be in the position of having a "helicopter view" of the WSS status quo.
	ANA should devise and promote policies which incentivise sub-national authorities to pursue investment projects from a

	regional, rather than local perspective.
Plan infrastructure and involve the private sector in WSS	The key responsibility of ANA on the creation of reference standards should be delivered as to consider policies that incentivise the sub-national authorities to seek private investment. In this process, ANA can learn much more from other national agencies, such as ANEEL (the electricity regulator).
	In the context of ANA and of the new Sanitation Law, the OECD Recommendations on the Governance of Infrastructure can be applied using the following elements: a. identifying policy goals, and evaluating whether regulation is necessary and how it can be most effective and efficient in achieving those goals b. considering means other than regulation and identifying the trade-offs of the different approaches analysed to identify the best approach c. supporting coordination between supranational, national and sub-national regulatory frameworks d. providing evidence-based tools for regulatory decisions, including stakeholder engagement, economic, fiscal, social and environmental impact assessment, audit and ex post evaluation e. conducting systematic reviews of existing regulation relevant to infrastructure, including consideration of costs and benefits, to ensure that regulations are up to date, costs are justified, effective and consistent, and that they deliver the intended policy objectives
	promoting good governance of regulatory agencies to ensure sustainable tariff setting, overall regulatory quality, and greater confidence from the market, and contribution to achievement of policy goals (e.g., independence, transparency, accountability, scope of action, enforcement, capacity and resourcing).
Understand finance providers' perspectives	A dialogue among relevant stakeholders, especially the providers of private finance, is needed to understand the challenges that the current framework poses for the investors. This would highlight whether the financial framework is fit for the purposes and needs of WSS investment, and could flag areas beyond WSS policy that the federal government needs to consider.
	The harmonisation and stability of the regulatory and WSS contractual framework brought by ANA's reference standards will be key in attracting new investment.
	Public acceptance of private investment in WSS will be noted both at the level of service provision, as well as by the end consumers. ANA should work on raising awareness to these stakeholder groups on the short- and long-term benefits of private investment. As Professor Berg noted in the slide deck for workshop week 19-22 October, the citizens "need to be confident that the system works for them".

Notes

[1] Law 14.026 of 15 July 2020, Article 11-B.

[2] Article 8, Paragraph 2, Law 14.026 of 15 July 2020: "For the purposes of this Law, regional basic sanitation units must be economically and financially sustainable and preferably include at least 1 (one) metropolitan region, and may be established by sanitation service granting authorities".

[3] Article 13, Law 14.026 of 15 July 2020.

[4] Article 4-A, Paragraph 3V, Law 14.026 of 15 July 2020.

Annex A. List of stakeholders consulted during the workshops

INSTITUTION	NAME
ABCON - Associação Brasileira das Concessionárias Privadas de Serviços Públicos de Água e Esgoto (Brazilian Association of Private Concessionaires of Public Services for Water and Sewage)	Percy Soares Neto
ABDIB – Associação Brasileira da Infraestrutura e Indústrias de Base (Brazilian Association of Infrastructure Industries)	Venilton Tadini
ABES – Associação Brasileira de Engenharia Sanitária e Ambiental (Brazilian Association of Water, Sanitation and Environmental Engineering)	Alceu Guérios Bittencourt
ABRHidro - Associação Brasileira de Recursos Hídricos (Brazilian Water Resource Association)	Synara Aparecida Olendzki Broch
AESA – Agência Executiva de Águas do Estado da Paraíba (Paraíba Water Management Executive Agency)	Ana Emília Duarte Paiva Bianca Azevedo Joacy Mendes João Pedro Chaves Da Silva Lovania Maria Werlang Magda Dayse Ferreira Rangel Marie Eugénie Malzac Porfírio Catão Cartaxo Loureiro
AESBE – Associação Brasileira das Empresas Estaduais de Saneamento (Brazilian Association of State WSS Public Operators)	Antônio Costa Lima Júnior
ADASA - Agência Reguladora de Águas, Energia e Saneamento do Distrito Federal (Regulatory Agency for Water, Power and Sanitation of the Federal District)	Jorge Enoch Furquim Werneck Lima
Agence de l'eau Adour-Garonne (Water Agency Adour-Garonne)	Sandrine Dupuis
AGER - Agência Reguladora de SINOP (SINOP Regulatory Agency)	Rayla Rocha
AGESAN RS - Agência Reguladora Intermunicipal de Saneamento do Rio Grande do Sul (Intermunicipal Sanitation Regulatory Agency of Rio Grande do Sul)	Daniela Rocke
ARES PCJ - Agência Reguladora PCJ (PCJ Regulatory Agency)	Dalto Favero Brochi
ARIS SC- Agência Reguladora Intermunicipal de Saneamento de Santa Catarina (Intermunicipal Sanitation Regulatory Agency of Santa Catarina)	Adir Faccio
TWRA - Aliança Tropical das Águas na Paraíba (Tropical Waters Alliance in Paraíba)	José Etham
ANA - Agência Nacional de Águas e Saneamento Básico (National Water and Sanitation Agency)	Alan Vaz Lopes Alexandre Anderáos Ana Carolina De Macedo Braz Ana Cristina Santos Strava Correa Ana Lucia Lima Barros Dolabela Ana Paula Fioreze André Cesar Moura Onzi Andre Raymundo Pante Beatrice Kassar Do Valle Bolivar Antunes Matos Bruno Collischon Carlos Motta

Carlos Perdigão
Christianne Dias Ferreira
Cintia Leal Marinho De Araujo Chagas
Cláudia Montenegro Silva
Claudia Fernanda Das Neves Oliveira
Claudio Ritti Itaborahy
Cristianny Villela Teixeira
Cristiano Caria Guimaraes Pereira
Edgar Gaya Banks Machado
Eliana Adjuto Botelho
Elizabeth Siqueira Juliatto
Eurides De Oliveira
Fabricio Vieira
Fernanda Abreu Oliveira De Souza
Flavia Carneiro Da Cunha Oliveira
Flavia Gomes Barros
Flávio Tröguer
Flávio José D'castro Filho
Gonzalo Vazquez Fernandez
Grace Benfica Matos
Humberto Cardoso Gonçalves
Iracema Aparecida Siqueira Freitas
João Augusto De Pessoa
Joaquim Guedes Correa Godim Filho
Jonilton Lima Torres
José Luiz Gomes Zoby
Leandro Mendes Da Silva
Leonardo de Almeira
Luciana Sarmento
Luis André Muniz
Luiz Henrique Amorim Moura
Marcelo Costa
Marcelo Mazzola
Marcelo Pires Da Costa
Marcelo Jorge Medeiros
Marco Antônio Mota Amorim
Marco Antônio Silva
Marcos Airton De Sousa Freitas
Maria Elisa Leite
Mariana Schneider
Michael Douglas Sanches
Nádia Eleutério De Souza Menegaz
Nazareno Marques De Araujo
Oscar De Moraes Cordeiro Netto
Osman Fernandes Da Silva
Patrick Thadeu Thomas
Paulo Augusto Cunha Libanio
Paulo Henrique Monteiro Daroz
Raylton Alves
Renata Lúcia Medeiros De Albuquerque
Ricardo Andrade
Ricardo Brasil Choueri
Rodrigo De Almeida
Rodrigo Flecha
Rogerio De Abreu Menescal
Rosana Mendes Evangelista
Sergio Ricardo Toledo Salgado
Sérgio Barbosa
Sérgio Rodrigues Ayrimoraes Soares
Taciana Neto Leme

	Tânia Regina Dias Da Silva
	Tauana Monteiro Guedes Do Santos
	Thamiris De Oliveiras Lima
	Thiago Gil Barreto Barros
	Tibério Magalhães Pinheiro
	Tomé Farias Siqueira Leitão
	Victor Eduardo De Almeida Saback
	Volney Zanardi Junior
	Wesley Gabrieli De Souza
APAC - Agência Pernambucana de Águas e Clima (Water and Climate Agency of Pernambuco State)	Clenio De Oliveira Torres Filho Crystianne Rosal Erik Cavalcanti E Silva Hélvio Ferreira Maria Lorenzza Pinheiro Leite Renata Pinheiro Robertson Valério De Paiva Fontes Suzana Maria Gico Lima Montenegro Tadeu Montenegro De Miranda Henriques
ARCE - Agência Reguladora de Serviços Públicos Delegados do Estado do Ceará (Regulatory Agency for Delegated Public Services of the State of Ceará)	Alceu Galvão
ASSEMAE – Associação Nacional dos Serviços Municipais de Saneamento (Brazilian Association of Municipal WSS Public Operators)	Aparecido Hojaij
Azevedo Sette Advogados (Azevedo Sette Lawyers)	Cynthia Cardoso
BID - Banco Interamericano de Desenvolvimento (Inter-American Development Bank)	Gustavo Mendez Sergio Campos
BNB - Banco do Nordeste (Bank of the Northeast)	José Wandemberg Rodrigues Almeida
BNDES – Banco Nacional do Desenvolvimento Econômico e Social (Brazilian Development Bank)	Guilherme Albuquerque Laura Bedeschi Letícia Barbosa Pimentel Marcio Zeraik
CAERN - Companhia de Águas e Esgotos do Rio Grande do Norte (Water and Sewage Company of Rio Grande do Norte)	Maria Geny Formiga De Farias
CAESB - Companhia de Saneamento Ambiental do Distrito Federal (Environmental Sanitation Company of the Federal District)	Aline Batista de Oliveira
CAGEPA - Companhia de Água e Esgotos da Paraíba (Water and Sewage Company of Paraíba)	Marcus Vinicius Fernandes Neves
Caixa Econômica Federal	Alexandre Honório Cayres Tatiana Thomé de Oliveira
Câmara dos Deputados (House of Representatives)	Deputado Enrico Misasi Deputado Evair Vieira de Melo Deputado Fernando Monteiro Deputado Geninho Zuliani
CGH ARG - Central Geradora Hidrelétrica Armando Ribeiro Gonçalves (Armando Ribeiro Gonçalves Hydroelectric Power Plant)	Adriano Divino de Sousa
Casa Civil da Presidência da República (Civil House of the Presidency of the Republic)	André Arantes Luciano
CNM - Confederação Nacional de Municípios (National Confederation of Municipalities)	Claudia Lins
COBRAPE - Companhia Brasileira de Projetos e Empreendimentos (Brazilian Company of Projects and Enterprises)	Luis Christoff
COPASA – Companhia de Saneamento de Minas Gerais (Sanitation Company of Minas Gerais)	Brigida Bueno Maiolini
CGU - Controladoria Geral da União (Office of the General Comptroller)	Carlos Ruchiga Marlos Santos

Organization	Name
CODEVASF - Companhia de Desenvolvimento dos Vales do São Francisco e do Parnaíba (Development Company of the São Francisco and Parnaíba River's Valley)	Luciano Campitelli Conti Salatiel Alves Coutinho Neto Sergio Luiz Soares de Souza Costa
COGERH - Companhia de Gestão dos Recursos Hídricos do Estado do Ceará (Water Management Company of Ceará)	Antonio Treze De Melo Lima Carla Fabiana Mont-Morency G. Rodrigues Denilson Fidelis Elano Joca José Martins De Andrade Marcelo Bezerra Marcilio Caetano De Oliveira Rafael Bezerra Tavares Vasques Landim Roberto Bruno Moreira Rebouças
COPPE - Instituto Alberto Luiz Coimbra de Pós-Graduação e Pesquisa em Engenharia da UFRJ (Alberto Luiz Coimbra Institute for Graduate Studies and Research in Engineering at UFRJ)	Jerson Kelman
DESO - Companhia de Saneamento de Sergipe (Sergipe Sanitation Company)	Andre Luis Pereira Oliveira
DNOCS - Departamento Nacional de Obras Contra as Secas (National Department of Infrastructure against Drought)	Alberto Batista
EJA - Faculdade Monteiro Lobato (Monteiro Lobato Faculty)	Patrícia Moreira Cardoso
EMATER Cajazeiras – Empresa de Assistência Técnica e Extensão Rural (Technical Assistance and Rural Extension Company)	Zildo Vicente Leite
Emparn/RN - Instituto de Pesquisa Científica em Parnamirim, Rio Grande do Norte (Scientific Research Institute in Parnamirim, Rio Grande do Norte)	Nelson Cesio Fernandes Santos Santos
FinoAgro - Finobrasa Agroindustrial	Evanio Vieira
Governo do Estado de São Paulo (Government of the State of São Paulo)	Helio Luiz Castro
Governo do Estado do Amazonas (Government of the State of Amazonas)	Fabio Augusto Alho Da Costa
Governo do Estado do Piaui (Government of the State of Piaui)	Erick Elysio Reis Amorim
Gpeas Semiárido - Grupo de Pesquisa Semiárido Brasileiro (Brazilian Semi-arid Research Group)	Laize Dos Santos Rodrigues
IFPB - Instituto Federal da Paraiba (Federal Institute of Paraiba)	Artur Lourenço Cybelle Frazão C. Braga Salomão De Medeiros
IGARN - Instituto de Gestão da Água do Rio Grande do Norte (Water Management Institute of Rio Grande do Norte)	André Lucas Nunes Antonio Marozzi Righeto Francisco Auricélio
Independant Consulant	Martha Maria Fialho Romulo Macedo Rui Costa Marques Wladimir Ribeiro
IRGA - Instituto Rio Grandense do Arroz (Rio Grandense Rice Institute)	Ivo Mello
MDR - Ministério do Desenvolvimento Regional (Ministry of Regional Development)	Anderson Bezerra André Braga Galvão Silveira Carla Barroso Claudio Xavier Seefelder Filho Claudir Afonso Costa Cristiane Battiston Demetrios Christofidis Ernani Miranda Irani Braga João Mendes Rocha Neto Lucas Bischof Pian Oscálmi Porto Freitas

	Pedro Maranhão
	Rafael Eduardo Teza De Souza
	Rogério Marinho
	Sergio Costa
	Sergio Soares
	Veronica Sanchez Da Cruz Rio
ME - Ministério da Economia (Ministry of Economy)	Diego Botassio
	Diogo Mac Cord De Faria
	Ernani Kuhn
	Fabiano Mezadre Pompermayer
	Fábio Ono
	Gabriel Godofredo Fiuza De Bragança
	Manoel Renato
	Marcelo Pacheco Dos Guaranys
	Martha Seillier
	Raul Menezes Dos Santos
	Wesley Callegari Cardia
MME - Ministério de Minas e Energia (Ministry of Mines and Energy)	Bruno Eustáquio de Carvalho
NDB - New Development Bank of BRICS	Marcos Thadeu Abicalil
PPA - Comitê de Bacia (Basin Committee)	Cicero Aurélio Grangeiro Lima
	Emídio Gonçalves de Medeiros
	Francisco José Bernardino Bernardino
	Isalúcia Barros Cavalcanti Maia
	João Batista Alves
	José Procópio De Lucena
	Maria De Lourdes Santana
	Vera Maria Lucas Ribeiro
	Walace Oliviera
	Waldemir Fernandes De Azevedo
Profill Engenharia (Profill Engineering)	Carlos Bortoli
	Meiri Michita
	Paola Marques Kuele
SABESP - Companhia de Saneamento Básico do Estado de São Paulo (Basic Sanitation Company of the State of São Paulo)	Marcel Costa Sanches
SEMA-RS - Secretaria do Meio Ambiente e Infraestrutura do Rio Grande do Sul (Secretary of Environment and Infrastructure of Rio Grande do Sul)	Amanda Fadel
	Marcela Nectoux
	Paulo Renato Paim
SAMAE - Serviço Autônomo Municipal de Água e Esgoto de Caxias do Sul (Municipal Water and Sewage Service of Caxias do Sul)	Rossano Belladona
SEMARH - Rio Grande do Norte State Secretariat of Environment and Water Resources (Secretary of State for the Environment and Water Resources of Rio Grande do Norte)	Paulo Varela
	Hélder Oliveira de Araújo
SEINFRA - Secretaria de Estado de Infra-Estrutura de Pernambuco (Pernambuco State Secretariat of Infrastructure)	Simone Rosa da Silva
Senado Federal (Federal Senate)	Sen. Tasso Jereissati
SINDUSCON-MG - Sindicato da Indústria da Construção Civil (Construction Industry Union)	Fabio Ferreira
SINGREH - Sistema Nacional de Gerenciamento de Recursos Hídricos (National Water Resources Management System)	Volney Zarnadi Junior
SRH – Secretaria dos Recursos Hídricos (Ceará State Secretariat of Water Resources)	Adahil Pereira de Sena
	Francisco Teixeira
STJ - Superior Tribunal de Justiça (Superior Court of Justice)	Ministro Herman Benjamim
TCU - Tribunal de Contas da União (Brazilian Court of Audit)	Daniel Mansur de Oliveira
	Marcelo Orlandi Ribeiro
UERJ - Universidade do Estado do Rio de Janeiro	Rosa Maria Formiga Johnsson

(Rio de Janeiro State University)	
UFCG - Universidade Federal de Campina Grande (Federal University of Campina Grande)	Daniela De Freitas Lima Karoline Solange Borges Teobaldo Maycon Breno Macena Silva Paulo Abrantes De Oliveira Regina Maria Pereira Ruan Teixeira
UFRGS - Universidade Federal do Rio Grande do Sul (Federal University of Rio Grande do Sul)	Ana Dalcin Guilherme Marques Rúbia Tatiane Da Luz Silva
UFRN - Universidade Federal do Rio Grande do Norte (Federal University of Rio Grande do Norte)	Eric Mateus Dias Yonara Santos
U.S. Departament of the Treasury	Walter Kulakowski
World Bank	Gilberto Canali Gustavo Saltiel Juliana Garrido Paula Pedreira De Freitas De Oliveira Rita Cestti Stela Goldenstein Viviane Virgolim Zamian

www.ingramcontent.com/pod-product-compliance
Ingram Content Group UK Ltd.
Pitfield, Milton Keynes, MK11 3LW, UK
UKHW050413240426
12048UKWH00020B/1488